CO-ALA-254

# One Size Fits Most

## THE FUNNY SIDE OF "ORDINARY" LIFE

*by rachel gies*

© Copyright 2001 Fairburn Publishing Corporation

First Edition

All rights reserved. Reproduction in whole or part of any portion in any form without permission of the publisher is prohibited.

P.O. Box 1164
St. Charles, IL 60175

ISBN: 0-9709960-0-4

Library of Congress: 2001090973

Printed in the United States of America

Editing by Nancy Root Miller of RiverTree Wordsmith

Illustrated and Designed by Camin Potts

Typeset and Proofread by Marcia Lorenzen

**Graphic Liaisons LLC**
Located in Amherst and Waupaca, WI

# Dedication

*To the memory of my beloved husband, Larry,*
*who encouraged me*
*every step of the way.*

# CONTENTS

# Acknowledgments

I would like to thank my husband, Larry, and our two children for their constant support. Also, thanks to my brother and sister-in-law, Ben and Fran Swaab, who spurred me on to write in the first place.

I would also thank the staff of the **Press-Republican**, especially my editor, Kimberly Bazant, for giving me the opportunity to say my piece, week after week. Most of these columns are reprinted with permission from the **Press-Republican**, a publication of Liberty Suburban Chicago Newspapers. The remainder were written expressly for this book.

# Preface

Having been Rachel Gies' editor at the newspaper for only a few years, I have had the pleasure of discovering what her readers have known for quite a long time: that sitting down with one of her columns is like visiting with an old friend—there's a promise of laughter, camaraderie, and understanding that transcends the bounds of geography and social classes.

Ms. Gies doesn't take her readers on a journey of fantasy or romance, and her tales aren't intended to be read through rose-colored glasses. Hers are stories of the everyday, unique spins on the commonplace that impel us to answer her clever tales with the words: "Yeah, I know just what you mean."

Born and raised in Amsterdam, Holland, Rachel and her family came to America in 1960. Later, she met and married her husband in Rockford, Illinois. They spent twenty of their happiest years together in Mendota and later moved to St. Charles, Illinois. She quickly became acclimated to the American culture and began cultivating a special talent—putting pen to paper. It is this gift that attracts people, entertains and soothes and, by virtue of its honesty, also binds.

As you turn the pages of this book, absorb each selection as it was intended to be read—one slice at a time. You're sure to find a new friend, and quite possibly, a new way to look at the very ordinary.

*Kimberly Bazant*

# ONE SIZE FITS MOST

Yes, there is life after the holidays. I've stuffed myself by gobbling tons of food, and during that time, I naturally have acquired a truckload of unwanted baggage. Next comes Valentine's Day and my loved one will take me out for dinner at one of the local restaurants. And, of course, I must look like a million dollars, even though I only have a few bucks leftover from the previous holidays.

I'm going to make up my "what in the world am I going to do" list. It's too late for a diet, but there are a few emergency steps I can take. I want to buy that snappy, sexy, voluptuous dress that I've been drooling over at the mall.

Naturally the outfit I like was made for a flat-chested, no-hips, no-thighs, dinky-bunned lady who did not come from this planet. There is no way that I'm going to stuff the big bosom I've developed and nurtured over the years into that micro-elasticized piece of spandex. I've spent too many years overworking and abusing my poor body by raising the children. But still, I want to look great for my hubby at dinner.

**Here are some useful pointers from various clothing experts:** One clever trick is to buy your outfit at least two sizes too big. When you choose an outfit a couple of sizes bigger and swear to your friends you've lost weight, who would dare disagree? Your clothes would not only look looser, but you'd also feel much more comfortable in roomier clothes. Also, buy yourself a one-piece body stocking that fits like an orthopedic suit made for someone that needs to be put into traction. Or, buy an outfit that says, "One size fits most." What do these people mean by "fits

# One Size Fits Most

most"? Most arms? Most hips? Most body parts? I just love it when the manufacturers crank out those baggy tents and matching babushkas!

Men expect us to look great, but what about their appearance? These guys eat themselves senseless at parties, and still think they look macho, but sucking in their stomachs no longer does the trick. They certainly aren't going to snatch their wife's girdle or buy their shirts and pants "one size fits most."

I have let my hubby's pants out many times, and I don't mean out for a stroll around the block! I have taken several of his pants to a seamstress and had them made two sizes larger than when he bought them. They just don't sell "under the bellybutton" pants.

How many guys do you know who wear their pants below their stomachs? They don't have a trim waist any longer. Yet, they expect their women to have great looking bods, a flat stomach, terrific breasts, and a young-looking face. And then they tell their wives to watch it, because her tummy is showing in the dress she's wearing.

He's forgotten who carried their heirs—and does he remember that at birth, Junior weighed more than the Thanksgiving turkey? And does he also remember when he told you to eat well for the baby? "You're eating for two," he'd say.

And now he wants a Cindy Crawford clone to go to dinner with him?

Whenever I've gone to a party with lots of food, I always feel like a cholesterol magnet. Everything sticks to me.

So, while I'm plotting to look my best for Valentine's Day, and hoping my sweetheart will still love me and send me flowers and candy—I'll go and buy that dress I've tried on and squeezed into a dozen times. I'll buy that paneled panty harness to flatten my tummy, wishing that hubby will notice how tiny I look tonight.

I hope that he tells me to enjoy the chocolates. I'll have the rest of the year to recoup and whip my body back into shape for the next holiday.

# BEWARE!
# THE RELATIVES
# ARE COMING!

I just got the news! My relatives have just notified us they will be visiting! The house is going to be a bed and breakfast for the next few days.

The beds will have to be made, and rooms that haven't seen a dust mop for some time have to be tidied up. The spider webs in the corners will just have to be destroyed. Out comes the power-vac to suck up those creatures.

The putrid vase that Aunt Tilly gave us as a wedding gift will come out of the attic to be displayed on the coffee table.

The dining-room table will need the extra leaf, and I'll need to drag out the moth-balled linen tablecloth—or what's left of it! I'll just go out and buy a new one—now Aunt Tilly won't gripe about it and offer me her hand-knitted recycled tablecloth that was originally made before World War I.

Stocking up on food is a must. The grocery list is endless! (It's longer than Santa's beard.) After purchasing the groceries, the refrigerator is so loaded with food it has to work overtime. With the motor running on high speed it sounds as if it has been pro-grammed for a U2 concert.

I'll need to drag out the old dishes that we haven't seen in ages. Can you imagine I used to believe this china looked expensive? (I remember how long it took to save the stamps to get the floral patterned dishes.) When we were married (many mega years ago) that flower pattern was the "in thing." It has been so long the chipped ones can't be replaced anymore—unless someone is selling them at a garage sale!

I have to beg the kids to clean up their rooms, watch their

manners, and be kind to Uncle Fritz and Aunt Tilly. I explain these are elderly people and the kids' dirty words and new tricks should be saved for another time. I warn them that Aunt Tilly's heart is not as strong as it was a few years ago.

Now, I've got to get hubby ready for the visit. I promise him that I'll give up shopping for a month (while crossing my fingers behind my back) if he vows to come home on time, treat my family with respect, and keep the "old fogy" jokes to a minimum.

He, in turn, asks me to take his car in for a tune-up, get a car wash and wax, and let him go bowling with his buddies on my mother's birthday. I agree to let him have his bowling night, I make him swear to not stop at Big Molly's for a beer. The deal is made.

When the relatives arrive, I am surprised at the change that has taken place over the years. Was Aunt Tilly's hair this white the last time I saw her? Since when have the lines on her face gotten to look like a road map to Tempe, Arizona?

Poor Uncle Fritz must have gained at least 20 pounds, and that hairpiece he's wearing matches Alvin the parrot's feathers—sort of pinkish-orange. As he inches closer I pray that he doesn't try to smooch me on the mouth as he always tries to do. His tobacco-stained lips and teeth, perfumed by his rancid garlic breath, never did appeal to me.

Then there's Aunt Tilly and her red lips. My brothers hated her "lip smackers," as she called her kisses. She'd chase them around the house until she caught them. The boys usually claimed to have a bad cold, or the incurable "cooties" disease, but it never stopped Aunt Tilly! My brothers got their revenge on her though, when they emptied some of Toto's cat food into Aunt Tilly's mashed-up carrots. She said the food was great, and wanted to know Mom's secret recipe.

Finally—after about a week of my playing maid, chauffeur, and cook, they are going home! Praise the Lord!

Aunt Tilly can't believe how fast the time went by (pray tell!). Was she counting the days? I know I have been. The kids have become unruly and aren't keeping their promise to behave. As has their father—he must have stopped at Big Molly's, although he denies it. He said he was working late. Yeah, right!

The kids were up to their old shenanigans. Uncle Fritz spent the whole afternoon looking for his tobacco pouch. I finally forced the kids to tell where they hid it—and then I had to immediately call the plumber. Uncle Fritz was a mite cranky after that!

Aunt Tilly practically cracked a couple of teeth on a plastic toy mouse the kids had put in her iced tea. That was one heart attack she didn't have to fake!

Anyway, now they're gone and the house has become a "normal" place again. The kids can play their tricks on each other, and once more their rooms look *au naturel* (a.k.a. hog-slop retreat).

My hubby swears the only reason he was late the last few evenings was because he gave Mort-the-Mooch a ride home from the bowling alley.

Yep, having relatives camp out for a month is just peachy! Or was it only a week? Same difference! And the best part is putting all the "goodies" away—until next time!

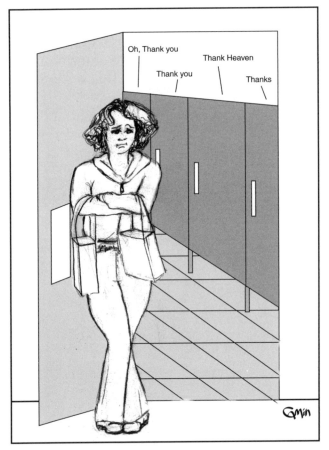

FRANTICALLY YOU SEARCH FOR THIS PLACE YOU NOW REFER TO AS HEAVEN. BECAUSE WHEN YOU FINALLY GET TO THE LADIES' ROOM, YOU LOOK UP AND SAY. "THANK HEAVEN."

# GOING TO
# THE MALL

Imagine you're at the shopping mall. All of a sudden a major emergency hits: You have to go the bathroom. But of course, the bathroom is eight blocks and ten light years away from where you are. Quickly, you run into the nearest store, a dress shop. You ask if you could please use their lavatory. The young clerk looks at you as if you asked her for free handouts. "Excuse me?" she asks. While you're crossing your legs in misery trying to hold back the urge, you repeat your request in plain English. "May I use your bathroom?" Your eyes plead for her understanding. She says, "Ma'am, you have to go to another store. Our bathroom facilities are private."

You want to yell that if you don't go in private, you may have to go public. But you want to keep your dignity. You explain to the young woman, who refuses to understand, that if she won't let you use the store potty, you will spill more than just your temper.

Still, she insists, "Our policy says we can't allow the public to use our facilities." (Sure, they think it is all right for us to spend our hard-earned money to support their business, but they won't let us do "our" business.)

Desperately you give up trying to reason with this person. Crawling toward the next shop, you pretend you're going to try on some outfits. The friendly clerk cheerfully tells you. "Take your time, I will start a dressing room for you." Good, now she will let you use the bathroom.

Hunched over in discomfort you ask, "Could I use your bathroom?" Looking at you as if you're trying to run off with the store's inventory she says, "Oh no. We have a policy, the

# One Size Fits Most

bathroom is off limits to our customers." "But I can't try on the clothes when I need to go to the bathroom," you argue. "Sorry, Ma'am, those are the rules."

You want to tell her what to do with the rules and the clothes, but you're in agony by this time. You leave, hoping the next store will grant you relief. While limping past sixteen more shops you finally spot a department store. You look all over the place for a clerk to direct you to the ladies' room.

At last you find a salesperson. You ask her where the bathroom is located. She tells you to go up three escalators into the men's department, take three turns to the left and two turns to the right. Mumbling your thanks while memorizing the directions, you stumble up the three escalators, following the clerk's instructions, and then end up at the wrong place.

Frantically you search for this place you now refer to as heaven. Because when you finally get to the ladies' room, you look up and say. "Thank heaven."

This was not the shopping trip you had in mind. You still haven't purchased a thing. You were spending your precious time trying to find a bathroom.

The question is—why should there be a problem for people to use a bathroom in a mall? Customers spend a lot of time in department stores and boutiques, yet, it is such a struggle for the public to use the bathrooms in these places. Some people may have bladder problems or may be pregnant. In instances like these, bathrooms are necessary. When a person has to walk clear across the mall to use the bathroom, that can really be a nuisance.

There must be a better way. Should all the stores have a public bathroom? The people who support these stores shouldn't have kidney failure while shopping.

But back in my hometown, where shop owners really know how to treat their customers, I talked to local shop owner. She says she has no problem letting her customers use her facilities while they're shopping.

Perhaps at the shopping malls there should be a "stop and shop porta-potty" inside the store near a dressing room, which has a sign that reads—

> # "Stop before you drop.
> # Our customers' wishes matter.
> # Please use our porta-potty
> # to relieve your swollen bladder."

CP

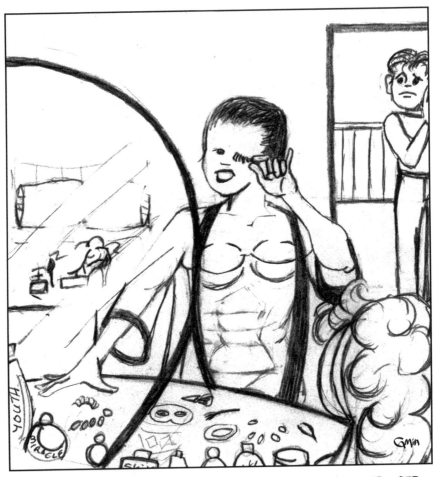

ERIC WATCHED IN HORROR AS SYLVIA REMOVED HER
HIGH HEELS, BLUE EYES, BLOND WIG, RED NAILS,
WHITE TEETH, FALSE EYELASHES,
AND FINALLY...
"NO!", HE PANICKED, "NOT THE..."
YES, HER FAKE BOOBS!

# WHAT'S AGE GOT TO DO WITH IT?

Did you ever say to someone? "Gee, you really look young. I hope I look as good as you do when I get to be your age."

Usually we treat people who are older than we are with a little more respect. We're happy helping elderly people walk across the street, and we willingly vacate our seat on a bus for an older person.

Are we worried about meeting up with Father Time? Do we see ourselves one day as that elderly person we helped crossing the street? What is it about aging that has all of us freaked out? We're a bunch of fad fanatics trying to hang onto our youth forever. We are scared of having to face the day when we will be senior citizens. Everything sold on the market is made to appeal to a younger generation. We're always trying to find ways that will keep us young forever.

The ads on TV and in magazines are all about how to maintain a younger look and how to take ten to fifteen years off our looks. We spend a fortune on the newest wrinkle creams—clogging up the pores on our faces. We slap on facial masks two to three times a week to firm up our skin. But, the only way to keep the skin from sagging is to keep the mask on or have a face-lift. We're stressing out by worrying how to stay slim and sexy for our partners.

Fashion companies constantly flash pictures of boys and girls who look about fourteen years old. Their make-up and clothes only look good on pencil-thin models, or a performance on the "Bozo, the Clown, Show".

Popular skin care products are promoted by models like

# One Size Fits Most

Claudia Schiffer and Cindy Crawford. Their perfect complexions sure didn't come out of a jar of facial cream. Kate Moss, the twiggy of the '90s, dominates the pages of fashion magazines wearing itsy-bitsy clothes.

Skinny forms mimicking Barbie dolls are demonstrating how you should pour your body into skin-tight jeans and spike-heeled shoes. Must we dress like models to feel and look sexy? How can we feel sexy after having stuffed our bodies into clothes made for someone who weighs less than 90 pounds? Who wears a size-2 outfit after age forty?

I don't recall Claudia, or Kate, giving birth to a baby. Mothers with babies living on a low budget don't have much time or money to get gussied up every day. They spend hours cleaning their homes, washing clothes, and taking care of their kids. (That's after they get home from work.) It is pretty hard to look like a fashion plate during breast-feeding sessions at 4:00 a.m.

The fashion world puts up signs and pictures on every billboard that say, "We'd better keep looking young and sexy if we want to hold on to our man." I wonder how these models have time to "hold on to a man" while they strut all over the world while hanging on to their breast implants. These girls are making millions doing their juggling, while we're struggling to keep up with our families. Many of us will never be rich or famous, but we'll try to grow old gracefully.

When at last you think you've achieved your goal by following every fashion trend and working out in the gym to keep in shape, you're about to enter the over-the-hill zone called "senior citizen."

Joining the crowd of people with arthritis and menopause syndrome, we realize aging is not the end of living, but an extension of a seasoned and more mature beginning. We discover we can still take part in doing all the things we did before. Such as exercising and looking our best. Cosmetic companies no longer have to convince us that we should look like we're thirty or forty forever.

When you celebrate your fortieth or fiftieth birthday with your friends, do you ever wonder if you look their age? When your friends tell you how great you look for your age, do you really believe them? Do you tell your friends how wonderful they look?

One thing is for sure—Father Time will put his final touches on us all, if we're lucky. Companies will compete by selling their latest over-the-counter feel-good gimmicks. We will most likely buy a few of the trinkets that make us look and feel better. Like Geritol for iron, and BENGAY® for our aches and pains. When we reach the golden-age stage, we'll spend some of our social security money for a few of the latest fads that promise us a longer life and a healthier tomorrow. Perhaps someone might say, "Wow, you look good for your age!"

# SHARING THE "BUG"

With the flu season at an all-time high you'd think that people would take better care to not spread their germs around. There is hardly a place to hide from the "bug." Standing in line at the grocery store sure is a great place to catch a virus. The lines are usually long and one can hardly escape a flu-infested crowd.

Many who have the "bug" are coughing, sneezing, honking their noses, and complaining how rotten they feel. If they are feeling so bad why do they stand around passing it on to you and me? Do they think we will thank them for spreading their bugs?

There are always some people who don't care if they spread their germs. And, you guessed it, eventually we'll be the recipients of the community bug.

Flu is like a pack of fleas; it jumps from one person to another—you can't shake or brush it off. Isn't it strange that Biffy, the cat, and Fido, the mutt, never seem to catch the flu? When have you seen animals carrying Kleenex® and nasal spray?

Children are the greatest bug spreaders. They usually catch everything and bring it home. Then they want to hug and kiss Mommy because they don't feel good. It seems this is one thing they don't mind sharing with the family.

How often do you go to a store and watch people sneeze in their hands, blow their nose in a paper tissue, and proceed to touch your groceries? When they bag your purchases, they wet their fingers to separate the plastic bags, and then they grab your food.

Church, or any public gathering, is usually another place to pick up a few extra bugs. People there spend the whole time

# One Size Fits Most

hacking and breathing down your neck. After the service or meeting, they want to shake your hand. I thought of wearing gloves, but the experts claim that washing your hands often is much more effective. Getting a flu shot isn't a sure thing either some people still get the flu after having the shot, but usually a milder form of it.

Finally, when the bug overtakes your body, you have to spend time nursing a miserable virus for days. Your head is pounding, your body aches and has the chills, and then there's the swollen glands that resemble golf balls. Not to mention phlegm-infested sinuses.

We can try some over-the-counter-medicine hoping it will help, but when we read all the dos and don'ts, we decide we're better off if we don't. Some side effects from the medicine are worse than the bug itself. Nothing seems to work, including the aching joints.

Finally, in desperation, we try Mother's old flu remedy and eat bowls of homemade chicken soup and spend hours over the vaporizer. The next few days will be spent lying around hoping to exterminate that bug.

When my family discovers I'm too sick to get up and fix their breakfast they are surprised. How could you get sick? Moms don't get sick—do they? When everyone is fed and dressed, Dad goes to work and the kids are off to school. Now I might get some well-deserved rest. No one will bother me until I'm well—I hope. Friends won't be calling thinking they might catch it over the phone. By the time I start to feel better I wonder when the virus will start bugging the rest of the family.

I still worry about those bug carriers walking around. When someone gets sick, shouldn't they stay home for a few days? Not only will they recover faster, they won't be spreading it to others. If people would stay home when they are sick, just think of how much you and I could save on time and flu medicine.

# PUPPIES LOVE

"Can we get a puppy, Mom? Joey got a new puppy for his birthday." I've heard this a hundred times. Sure I've told the kids dozens of times that having a pet takes a lot of time and responsibility. The animal would need a lot of attention and you have no time to care for it, I remind them.

The kids beg, plead, and try to wear me down. I know who'd be taking care of the puppy. Every unidentified living creature the kids brought along I fed and cleaned up after.

The kids promise on their honor, and pledge their undying love for this pet. Is this déjà vu from another time?

When I finally give my blessing, hoping these kids are mature enough to help raise a pet, the puppy comes home. Everybody "oohs" and "ahhs" over the darling little puppy. They'll take turns feeding the puppy, the kids vow. Their eyes are full of love, promise, and devotion. That was then.

After the novelty wore off, Mom is nominated to take care of the puppy while the kids are in school. Mom takes the time for puppy to get his shots and cleans up the messes. Dad stays neutral. He gets to play with the puppy and help pay the bills. When Dad tires of playing, he asks for those in charge to take the puppy outside. That is, oops, after puppy pooped.

Those who said, "We will care for the puppy as soon as we get home from school," didn't keep their end of the bargain. Sure, did I forget? I believed them when they said they'd take care of Todd the turtle, and Mackerel and Lew the two goldfish. Someone accidentally forgot to feed them.

Unfortunately they all joined one another in pet heaven. Along

# One Size Fits Most

with Morris the gerbil and Lizzi the lizard, who had previously been members of the family.

Paper training seemed sufficient for a while. Even Dad was helping by donating his weekly newspapers to the potty training. But before we knew it, someone conveniently forgot to take puppy out to do his business. I distinctly remembered the kids saying they would take care of the puppy. Now they're arguing about whose turn it is to take the poor thing out.

While everyone was deciding who opens the door to let him out, again, puppy just couldn't hold it waiting for their decision. I threaten that if no one takes care of the puppy, he will have to go. Once again I repeat the rules. But I know the only time the kids can help is after school. Of course, they have basketball, baseball, piano lessons, and homework.

After eating their meals, calling their friends for hours, and playing hard with puppy, it's time for bed. When I asked whose turn it is to feed puppy and take him out for the night, the kids remind me they have early classes and practice in the morning.

Well, that leaves just one person who had said that this puppy must go if no one takes care of him. When I protest that I don't have the time to take care of this puppy it is too late. Of course, I won't be able to part with this critter with his cute little snout. He has become a member of the family and my friend.

Besides, when I come home from a hard day at work he will be there to greet me. Who else can I trust with all my little secrets?

# RECYCLED BAGS

We all spend a lot of time recycling our garbage. This is the right thing to do in today's society. After all if we don't start taking care of our environment, we will be in a lot of trouble in the future.

Most of the people in and around my town are now separating their pop bottles from their garbage and placing these items in different containers.

But one can take things too far. For instance, some stores have decided to use old secondhand bags for your new merchandise. That can be a little disgusting. I've seen clerks actually put people's articles and clothes into a used, plastic bag! These bags previously held returned merchandise.

Watching the salesperson take my items and put them into an already used sack got me curious as to what this bag held before it was returned, to be reused.

I know what I have done with my plastic bags from stores. Charlie, my pooch, has had several accidents in the house, so these plastic bags sure came in handy when I disposed of his doo-doo. Also, I found that they are great for lining the garbage cans in our bathrooms, which saves me some money that I usually spend on garbage bags.

Messes in the kitchen are a snap to clean up with a small plastic bag. So why would one reuse a bag that had been returned to the store? When I return an item I will grab any old bag to return my stuff. Yet, I don't expect to return these bags only to have them used for someone else's purchases.

Lord only knows what kind of trash some bags may carry.

# One Size Fits Most

What's next, pre-owned bread bags? Will people stuff our bread loaves into somebody else's used bread bag? Or will we return our used meat package that contained hamburger?

One has to wonder about hygiene. With all the diseases that are being spread, and all the viruses lurking around, you wouldn't want to add more problems by having stores using old bags!

Recently, I went to a grocery store in the area, and really got angry. It really frosts me when some people are careless and don't have any consideration for their fellow humans. I was checking out the groceries at the counter, and the person bagging my things had a cold. Granted, we all are subject to catching the sniffles. But this person was bagging my food while he wiped his dripping nose, and his lips were encrusted with cold sores resembling rust spots! All the while he is handling my groceries and rubbing the germ-soaked tissue under his dripping nose! I wanted to grab those grocery bags and bag them myself.

When I made a remark to the checkout person, I was told to confront the nose-runner himself. Why should we, the customers, have to say anything at all? This should be taken care of by the management and not by the customers.

Still, I firmly believe in saving the earth and helping our next generation by cleaning up the environment. I also believe we need to educate people on health and hygiene to minimize the spread of germs.

I do not want anyone's returned garbage bags used for my purchases and spreading diseases.

# FACE-LIFT

Getting a face-lift reminds me of when I remodeled the house. Once you start working on one room you want to do a complete makeover.

People who decide to have plastic surgery on their faces might as well do their whole bodies. I can usually tell when someone has had too much surgery on her face.

When I see Barbara Walters and Joan Rivers on TV, they barely smile and hardly move their lips when they talk. Could it be their faces might crack? They both have had so many face-lifts they've captured that frozen CNN look. When did you see Barbara and Joan wearing a sleeveless outfit? They usually wear dressy suits with long sleeves to cover up their arms.

There must be times when you look in the mirror and wonder what it would be like to have a tummy tuck, or a little work on your face, or perhaps breast implants. Over the years we've been stuffing our stomach and rear end into firm control triple-panel briefs, and we've shoved our bosom into minimizer bras. We've also spent a fortune on anti-wrinkle potions and moisturizing lotions to keep our skin from sagging. If the majority of the people had the money, would they consider having surgery to make themselves look younger?

Sure, lots of movie stars have cosmetic surgery and have their bodies rearranged. They make their living trying to look forever young. Some of these characters might be the same age as I am. But as the years go by I'm the one who has aged and they still look like they did when I first saw them on the screen. Most stars

# One Size Fits Most

"fib" about their age and deny they ever had surgery. Even some of the male actors make my hubby look like someone's elderly uncle.

When I look at some of the female stars with processed hair, plumped breasts, and thighs that look sculpted by lots more than weight training, I just think that it must be awfully costly and time-consuming. The average person can't afford that kind of luxury. Besides, would your spouse be happy to see you look much younger than he?

Even if I could manage to scrape up the money for a face-lift, wouldn't my hubby prefer the rest of my body to match my much younger-looking face? Also, would my old body have enough zip left after the surgery to keep up with my newly sculpted cheek-bones?

When I worked in a beauty salon I knew a few people who had had reconstructive surgery. My boss, for one, decided to get a face-lift. She wanted to please her hubby. After she spent much of her savings and went through the pain, her sweet hubby ran off with her best friend who was six years older than she was.

Then there was a famous fan dancer by the name of Sally Rand who performed in our town years ago. When I met Sally she had to be in her sixties. But her face and body were fabulous. She looked like she was in her early forties. I was assigned to be her hairstylist at the time of her visit.

When I proceeded to shampoo her hair, I noticed the scars behind each of her ears. Sally was a very sweet and funny person and she told me about the many face-lifts she'd had. She joked as she showed the scars on her hands. She said she had to keep her hands, her face, and her body looking young because that's how she made her living.

Each night Sally performed her act on stage completely in the nude. People "barely" got a glimpse of her body as she moved gracefully around on the stage. Only her face and hands showed while her body was covered by her famous fans. No one was aware of the scars on her hands because they were hidden by the dim lights. Every few years Sally had to have more surgery to keep herself in that shape.

We all would like to look young forever. But at what cost? One wonders if it's worth going through all the trouble fooling with Mother Nature.

I guess I will have to keep my same old face and just give my body and spirits a lift buying a new body slimmer with heavy-duty tummy control. At least hubby won't have to worry about my spending his money on a "nip and tuck" and end up looking younger than he does.

MY MOTHER GETS INTO HALLOWEEN SO MUCH
IT'S KINDA SCARY!

# LET'S GET READY FOR HALLOWEEN

Halloween is coming. Witches and goblins are cruising out of their caves to ring doorbells and drive people batty for hours.

The young ones can't wait to perform their tricks while collecting their treats. Bags fill up with lots of goodies—ranging from candy to gooey taffy apples. Childrens' footsteps can be heard shuffling out on the front porches and sidewalks, anxiously awaiting their rewards.

The first year we lived here I bought enough candy to fill a school bus. I dressed to kill. When I thought I looked like the grandchild of Frankensteins' daughter, I was ready to face the little ghouls. My husband jumped when he saw me, and for the first time in our marriage he confessed that I looked truly ugly. Good, I thought with glee. When the dog saw me in my get-up, he barked until his vocal cords went into recess—the poor thing went into hiding for days.

I was ready and waiting for the doorbell to ring, and when it did I got so excited I almost dumped the whole bucket of candy in the little goblin's bag. I guess I must have really looked scary. He dropped his bag and ran off. Wasn't he supposed to scare me?

We waited for the next bunch to come. Finally another kid dared to come up to the door. He told us in a terror-filled voice that there was something weird sitting out on the lawn. Sure, I thought, this must be his trick. All right, we're game, we'll come and look.

It was an eerie night and being out in the country was certainly not like living downtown with bright lights. (Our outdoor

# One Size Fits Most

lights are very sparse, and it always looks a little haunted around here.)

When we walked outside, there was a life-size casket sitting on our lawn. Good grief, I though in panic, is this nuts? My husband, brave as he was, inched closer to the dusty, old coffin and started talking to it. Then suddenly the lid slowly creaked open, and creeping out of the casket was a long-fingered, withered hand with six-inch nails!

Then the rest of whatever was inside the coffin slithered out. I howled like a rabid wolf! I froze in fear when I noticed the thing was going to attack my husband. But suddenly, I realized the creature was hugging my husband, and he was hugging it back!

The "Thing" in the coffin turned out to be one of our good friends from our hometown, who decided we shouldn't be lonesome on our first Halloween away. These are friends? What kind of "friends" plant coffins on your front lawn and scare the stuffing out of you? So, after warding off the guys with straitjackets, and our blood pressure had stabilized, we finally had a good laugh.

We all had some ghoulish fun by going trick-or-treating. We begged our friends to leave the coffin for the next year, but they said they needed it to put "Quinten-the-mannequin" away for next year. He always sat on their front porch during Halloween. We rejoiced when our dog finally came out of hiding, (He is still a bit cautious around us.)

The following year I figured we wouldn't have many kids risking their lives to come out in this dark and spooky low-light area. Was I wrong!

By 7:00 that night I was making an emergency run to the store to buy more candy. When I got back, my husband was about to start giving away our household furnishings to keep the little monsters happy. Their tricks were much more threatening than I had imagined.

I rushed to the rescue with more candy in my arms. We happily shared the goodies with all the munchkins. For some reason I didn't scare off too many kids this year. Maybe because I had my own face on? The rest of the evening went quite smoothly.

# LET'S GET READY FOR HALLOWEEN

I wonder how this year will be? But no matter—we will be prepared for a fun-filled Halloween. . . and be assured, there will be plenty of treats—but no coffins!

# MY CREDIBILITY ALMOST WENT UP IN SMOKE

I remember the first day I tried to quit smoking. It would have been much easier for me to have won a polo match, or commit a major crime. But, I thought it would be better to try to give up cigarettes.

My kids hated my nasty habit, and often threatened to leave home. Many times I told them to go ahead and leave—but they convinced me that I needed their support, and that they weren't old enough to take care of themselves—pity!

The first few days I acted like I was pregnant again. I ate tons of pickles and prayed for strength. Days three through ten, I pigged out on mega doses of chocolates and gummy bears. By evening, I was so hyper from all the sweets I was yelling at the kids—who then begged me to start smoking again. They even offered to pack my suitcases.

Oddly enough, by day twenty, I could actually drink a cup of coffee and talk on the phone at the same time—without craving a cigarette. What an accomplishment, I thought!

After a month I noticed I could talk to the kids without yelling at them, and not accuse them of trying to prematurely dig me an early grave. I even said "hello" to my husband again, petted the dog, and let my friends take me out to lunch in public places.

When I went to the mall or grocery store, I found that I had a slight problem being around other smokers. I would follow second-hand smoke around like a hungry mutt following the aroma of raw steak. I would sneak up behind the smokers and inhale deeply. Then I was caught sucking up their exhaled smoke, because they noticed they were being trailed by a "nut on the loose."

But other than that small mishap, I was doing quite well. My husband promised he would stop smoking in a few months if I kept with the program. (He thought I wouldn't make it through the month.)

I did fall off the smoke stack—so to speak. One time I just had to sneak one little puff. I was sure the kids would never know. I had gone into the bathroom, locked the door, and lit up a cigarette I had snuck from my hubby's stash. He wouldn't miss one little "ciggy." I had opened the window slightly so the smoke would have a quick escape. No one would be able to smell a thing.

Wrong! I snapped out of my blissful smoking coma when I heard a sound I had prayed I wouldn't hear.

"Mommy! You lied!" Two accusing voices announced. One would have thought I was Lizzie Borden being accused of murder!

Outside the window were my two darlings who must have seen my smoke signals coming from the window. These are the kids I had given birth to—they should've been grateful I gave them life, but they wouldn't even let me have a measly puff! These two rug rats were scolding and betraying their own mother! I felt both guilty and embarrassed for getting caught by those little crunch-munchers. I'd never hear the end of this, I thought.

"We're gonna tell Dad when he gets home," they lisped in unison. Where did they hear that phrase before?

I begged for their forgiveness. My daughter was forgiving after I promised I'd never take a puff again, and that I would buy her a new wardrobe. My son was harder to convince, however. I needed to earn his trust again. He said if I didn't smoke for an entire year, he would again have faith in his mom.

For months I ate carrot sticks, celery, and fruits. I feared that extra blubber would attach itself to my body once I gave up smoking. My friends provided me with diet books and self-help tapes. These are friends?

Even though it was a tough fight to quit, I am grateful to my family and friends. Without their support it would really have been a long battle. They kept telling me I looked so much better since I was no longer puffing on those cigarettes, and that my wrinkles seemed less noticeable. Gee—how ugly was I?

Quitting was probably one of the hardest things I have ever had to do—besides learning how to cook and save money, that is! But it has been rewarding. My kids still love me, and my friends let me visit *inside* their homes.

I think it has been about 12 years since I quit—or has it been 20 years? I'm not sure. It has been said that if you aren't exactly sure when you quit smoking—you're cured!

## One Size Fits Most

# GRANNIES

I was listening to the radio and someone was talking about the two grandmothers who were coming to the United States to see the little Cuban boy, Elian Gonzales. Something about that conversation struck me. One talk show host was referring to these two women as "grannies."

Normally I wouldn't have given this subject much thought. But I wonder when we think of grandparents, does that mean these are old people who have to lean on a cane to stand up and clutch an oxygen tank to their bosom to catch their breath? Does being a grandparent make us think of Aunt Bea from the "Andy Griffith Show"? Or Granny from the "Beverly Hillbillies" making her homemade brew? Do we picture Grandpa waiting by the mailbox in a wheelchair for his social security check?

There are lots of grandparents who don't look, or act, like "old geezers." They are in great shape and look very youthful. Think of stars like Loni Anderson, Raquel Welch, Roger Moore, and Sean Connery. Not all grandparents look like movie stars, but some grandparents look ageless. When I was a teenager, I used to think folks over 25 were ancient.

For the last several decades, grandparents have gone through a big change. This includes good health care plans, a more positive outlook on aging, and a more daring approach to fashion. Many people over 50 dress youthfully and keep a close watch on their diets by eating lots of nutritious foods. They also spend time working out at the health clubs, and walking miles in shopping malls.

Grannies and grandpas no longer fit that "old fogey" mold.

# One Size Fits Most

They don't sit in their rockers listening to slow music, they go out and rock! When people retire they don't stay home eating oatmeal and adjusting their dentures. Many more retirees crave to go and travel the continent for excitement. It has been said that age is mind over matter. If you don't mind, it doesn't matter.

A member of my family is spending her retirement traveling all over Europe. She is a terrific-looking grandmother and recently celebrated her 74th birthday. My mother-in-law, at the age of 83, has traveled on many bus tours to different states and is still going. Nowadays, grandmothers are even having babies and nobody is shocked.

A few years ago I was watching a program on TV. The host of the show was about to introduce some well-known authors. When the two authors—under the pen name of Fern Michaels—came out, I did a double take. Imagine the surprise when two elderly females showed up for the interview. They have been writing the steamiest, sexiest stories for years.

Some people wait to do their thing after they have raised their family. When they finally have the time and courage to pursue their interests perhaps they can make their wishes come true.

A couple I knew had waited their whole lives to fulfill their dream. They wanted to be with their children who had immigrated to America. They had lived through a frightening war and were terrified that their remaining children would be subjected to the horrors of yet another war. Though these people had never traveled beyond their own country, they decided to make the ultimate sacrifice. They gave up the business they had owned for more than 40 years and left their homeland in pursuit of a new life. At the ages of 56 and 67, the couple and their two younger children immigrated to America. There they would start a new venture in the land of the free, and spend their remaining years with all their children and grandchildren.

# GOING ON VACATION

It is just about time for the kids to go back to school. The rush is on trying to get them ready.

I remember when the kids were little and we were planning our vacation. It all seemed so simple. The only thing I had to do was pack Dad's and the kids' things and make arrangements for the goldfish and cats. Fido would accompany us on the trip. A friend offered to look after the mail and delivery of the newspaper. I made sure we had enough toys, games, and snacks to keep the little ones occupied for the duration of the long drive to Grandma's house.

Sure, once we got to Grandma's everything would be great. After all, it was a relief not having to take Fido for a walk in the woods and afterwards having to pick off the burrs that had gotten stuck in his fur, and clean his mud-soaked paws.

Of course, there was the carsickness that snuck up so suddenly. I had given them a dose of DRAMAMINE® hours earlier—the ad read "Barf-free trips"—so what happened? Cleaning up Dad's nice shiny car did not add to the vacation fun.

After hours of driving, with whining, hungry loved ones, the restroom and eating stops seemed like a gift from heaven. After gassing up the wagon and feeding Fido, off we went to complete the journey to Grandma's.

Many potty stops later we arrived, and the kids literally adopted their grandparents as their legal guardians since their parents had forced them to sit still for hours in the car, endure motion sickness, and eat real food for their sick tummies. Grandma's chicken and mashed potatoes made everyone forget the long

# One Size Fits Most

trip. Settling the upset tummies and feeding Fido the leftovers from everyone's plates felt like Christmas.

After the young ones had been put to bed, it was time for the grown-ups to relax. But not so fast. The rest of the relatives showed up and brought all the cousins to show Aunt Dora and Uncle Fletch how much the darlings have grown. "Gee, wasn't Rupert still in dydees when you last visited?" And "You didn't know that Molly had her first communion last year?" Wondering where the time has gone, I pull out all of my favorite pictures and get the kids out of bed to see their cousins. Some have grown so much the kids barely recognize each other. Soon the kids are bonding and talking. The visits with the family are great, but I'm longing for some rest—or so I thought! Plans are being made for the duration of our stay—going to people's homes, and countless picnics.

At last it's time to go home. Do up the laundry and pack the bags for the trip. Aunt Minnie gave me her homemade concoction for carsickness. It looks awful, but Aunt Minnie swears it will work. She said she used it on the cows when they were sent to market. I decided to use the medicine the pharmacist had recommended!

What a sense of relief when we finally pulled into our driveway. Home at last! Now the kids will be going back to school, and their dad will be going back to work, and maybe I can get a little vacation time of my own. Am I dreaming?

The dream has just vanished as the kids holler, "Mom, where are my school clothes?" My vacation has gone by the wayside. There is cooking and laundry, grocery shopping, and registering the kids for school. Let's see, what could possibly be left for me to do? Maybe I can get a real vacation!

# WHAT IS MY STYLE?

When I browse through the pages of fashion magazines, it seems that models appear like Barbie look-alikes on a food-fasting binge! I truly wonder about the young girls today who diet themselves into skin and bones to become a model. Their jobs are to sell our kids everything from the latest fads in dieting to how to apply cosmetics, and show off the latest trend in clothes.

In these pictures, models are shown wearing skin-tight pants and tops, designed to impress men! Some of the models look as if they borrowed Bozo the Clown's makeup kit from Tammy Fay Baker.

Now the magazines are splashing photos of young women, showing an alluring look for lips and breasts, created from collagen injections and saline-filled breast implants. To think that teenagers actually want to look like these creatures!

They want a slim body and large breasts. Just take a look at Pamela Anderson Lee and Anna Nicole Smith. These women are at least eight dress sizes apart, and both women have enormous bosoms to lug around.

Pamela's breast implants made her look as if she might topple over. At least Anna Nicole is well proportioned throughout her entire body.

You wonder what is going through people's minds when they choose their role models. Do teens really believe it is worth risking their health by starving their bodies into a size-2 dress, or pouring themselves into a pair of jeans that fit so snugly it cuts off their circulation? Do young men really want girls looking like scarecrows with implants?

# One Size Fits Most

Teenage models are offered big bucks for keeping their bodies anorexic to pose for magazines. I wonder what they eat to exist. Perhaps a thimble filled with cereal for breakfast, and a glass of water? In *Cosmopolitan* magazine there was an article claiming that one of their top models eats two lettuce leaves for lunch! I inhale more calories when I take a breath of air! For me, oxygen isn't even calorie-free.

Teenagers have enough to worry about; they shouldn't need fashion magazines telling them they need to look like a piece of vermicelli strapped into spandex.

This reminds me of the '60s, when a young girl came into the fashion world and became an overnight sensation. Her name was Twiggy. I remember one of my friends was dying to look like Twiggy. She nearly succeeded too, by starving.

Of course, I also wanted to model myself after this phenomenon, thinking men would adore me and drop themselves at my feet.

I guess I survived the Twiggy wanna-be era, but the pressure that young girls are under today to look thin is a lot tougher than it used to be.

The fashion world has always tried to dictate what women should wear. They design styles and tag on prices that many women can't afford. They keep running ads trying to convince teenagers that if they weight 90 pounds, wear layers of makeup, and dress like an object resembling a broomstick swaddled in cloth, they're making a statement.

If designers want to sell a clothing line, they need to cater to more seasoned women with some character to their faces and bodies. They must also design styles with some room so young girls don't have to stop eating. Perhaps they might allow a little extra material for the more mature woman? I may no longer have a size-3 outfit in my closet, and I might not fit into my old yellowed wedding gown anymore, but I know that whenever I look into a mirror, my gravity-pulled, sagging body certainly fits into *my* lifestyle.

# PERMANENT BILLS FOR A TEMPORARY CROWN

I recently visited my dentist for a checkup and cleaning. When I walked into the office, I was greeted by the bubbly assistant who then escorted me to the torture chamber. "Sit down and relax, we'll take some X-rays before the doctor looks at your teeth," she said with a smile. "Aren't X-rays dangerous?" I ask the assistant. She says "No," and quickly hides behind the door to take the X-rays of my teeth! If it isn't dangerous, then why is she hiding behind the door? But, I assure myself, she does this a dozen times a day, every day, and I only get it twice a year.

After that was done she spent the next 15 minutes probing and scraping my teeth. When the final polish was completed, the doctor walked in. "And how are we today?" What does he mean "we"? I'm the one having my gums and lips mauled.

While he was checking the X-rays, he frowned and mumbled something that sounded like, "You need a crown." I don't believe he means the kind Miss America wears. He shows the X-rays to me (as if I'm supposed to know what to look for). All I see are these big black things and white objects that look like tumors.

He continued by telling me my gums are beginning to recede—so is my husband's hairline! He pointed out the trou-bled spots on the white part. They look like Mr. Ed's teeth to me.

"Well," I carefully asked him, "what are you suggesting?" He studied my face as if considering reconstructive surgery. All the while I was seeing dollar signs flashing in his eyes. "You need treatment to help heal those troubled spots."

"Treatment!" I mimicked. (Easy for him to say.) "Will it hurt much?" I quivered.

# One Size Fits Most

"Nah, you'll be just fine. We'll numb the gums and it'll be as if your mouth is taking a snooze," he joked. He produces a foot-long needle to stick in my mouth, as he good-naturedly chatted about his family—expecting me to answer questions—but I was afraid to respond because his needle might slip.

Meanwhile, my swollen, numbed tongue is lolling out of the side of my mouth. All I can do is grunt and agree with him.

The assistant handed me an extra napkin and I mumbled, "thanks," while trying to control my facial muscles to keep my tongue behind my inflated lips. Finally, he was through.

Thanking God, I'm ready to go home. Doc said, "We'll see you in two weeks."

"What?" I slurred.

"This is only a temporary crown," he explained. "The permanent one will be ready to be inserted in two weeks."

"Oh," I said—wondering what excuses I can think of—at least Miss America gets to wear her crown for a year. As if reading my mind he said, "Now, don't put this off, this is very important."

"All right," I agreed, reluctantly.

"By the way, here is your lollipop for being such a good patient," Doc said, "until next time—pleasant dreams."

# AMERICA, THE BEAUTIFUL?

I'm driving along the highway, and suddenly I see something flying through the air and it splatters all over my car. My vehicle has just been christened with someone's leftover lunch! To say I was feeling outraged is an understatement, especially since I just had my car washed.

There isn't much I can do about these litterbugs who discard their garbage on the roads. They commit these acts and couldn't care less about my vehicle or my property. Some people assume that the roads are dumping grounds for garbage.

We're told to clean up this and recycle that to help save the earth from being trashed. Millions of dollars are spent each year to find ways to keep this country clean and healthy for future generations. There are signs all across the country that say "Keep America Beautiful."

When I see some careless bozo throwing a burning cigarette butt out of a car, I do a slow burn. How many times have you waited at a stoplight and watched someone ahead of you open a car door and dump out an ashtray? What's worse is while you wait for the light to change, someone opens his car door to spit out a wad of chewing tobacco.

Also, have you noticed the piles of baby diapers lying around the parking lots? People like cleaning out their car right in the parking lot. When I leave a store and see trash next to my car I hate to think that someone has thought the trash belonged to me.

Needless to say, these inconsiderate dolts who think nothing of tossing diapers and cigarette butts next to my car would be rendered apoplectic if somebody dumped the stuff on their

# One Size Fits Most

driveway. I was recently driving on the highway and was shocked at the amount of garbage lying alongside the road.

In the last few years I have made it a point to sort through my stinky garbage to sort and divide papers, bottles, and cans before I take out the trash. Neighbors who walk their pet carry a pooper-scooper, and a Ziploc® baggy to pick up Fido's splatter-matter. Most people really keep their yards and streets clean. But it frosts me when there is a bunch of empty beer bottles and food containers spread out in people's yards left by careless passersby. Talk about drinking and driving! Usually one of the neighbors will pick up the empties and put them in their garbage can.

Someone literally threw out a kitchen sink from a moving motor home while I was on my way to a neighboring town one day. It barely missed the cars driving behind the vehicle and landed on the side of the highway.

Fortunately, here in my neighborhood, most people enjoy living in a clean and healthy environment. There is a lot of pride in keeping our area well maintained.

During our local festivals people work hard to make the cities presentable, there were a lot of extra garbage containers on the streets and most people made use of them. But there were a few who didn't.

If someone plans to use our cities as a dumping pit I hope they will remember the song from 1895, "America The Beautiful." *(Words by lyricist, Katherine Lee Bates, and music by composer Samuel A. Ward.)*

# A
# STACKED
# DECK

When I conducted my annual "clean out my overloaded hand-bag," I realized that besides having every beauty product and face gadget ever made in my handbag, I also carried a ton of credit, membership, and discount cards with me. No wonder my shoulders ached after my shopping trips.

I decided to find out just how many cards I owned. I was shocked as I dug up an assortment of cards from all sorts of places. Among them I discovered several video store cards from places that are no longer around. I had preferred customer cards from every grocery store in the area. I pulled out my gas station card, frequent movie-goer card, and several VISA cards. I also had bunches of colorful credit cards from every department store within 20 minutes of my home (and beyond). I had even saved a library card from the early '80s.

Just how many cards did I have? When I dumped out all the stuff from my wallet, to my astonishment, there were over 50 credit, membership, service, affinity, and discount cards. I almost had a full deck! I decided to play my cards right and cut up the ones I didn't need. Now I was beginning to feel a weight being lifted from my shoulders (literally).

Then a few weeks ago my husband handed me another card—from the car wash—so I could take advantage of the discount on my next trip there. Saving money sounded good to me, so I tucked away my newly acquired saving's privilege. Then I was offered yet another saver's card at the mall's coffee shop. Every time you order a cup of coffee they will punch your card. When the card is full, you get a free cup of coffee. I accepted the card

# One Size Fits Most

since I love the thought of a free cup of coffee. When I was handed a donut card from a local grocery store I was tempted. The thought of free donuts was hard to resist. Due to the holiday ten pounds that I had gained, the jury is still out on that scrumptious card! It occurred to me that I was a magnet for membership, "free" credit, bargains, and freebies. I knew that eventually my handbag would again be overloaded with a fresh deck of colorful plastic.

Well, that leads me to the point of all this. Aren't credit cards supposed to be for convenience? Have you ever traveled with a road warrior on a long trip? The dazzling array of multiple "frequent this" and "frequent that" cards used makes my head spin. There's a card for the airline, a card for the rental car, one for the hotel, and a discount card for upgrades on the way home. How about the different levels of membership—you have gold, platinum, and silver—is uranium next?

Recently at the grocery store, the first thing the checkout person asked was for my preferred card so that I could get my discount. I thought—would I not be a preferred customer without the card? Well, I dug through my purse while putting my items on the counter. Once I had located it, the card was swiped through a scanner. That done, I tucked away my preferred card, pulled out the coupons I clipped from the newspapers and proceeded to write a check. The checkout person needed to see my card again to process my check, then swipe it through the scanner which, of course, had to be repeated several times until the machine read my over-used card. The bad news is that the line behind me became longer and more frustrated at my record-setting check out.

Now the banks have come out with a revolutionary debit card. It is marketed as the most important peace of mind one can have. Upon inquiry, I found out that instead of getting one month of grace like most credit cards, this intrusive treasure takes money directly out of my account—that minute! This is certainly not convenient for me!

I wonder—with all these cards are we really accomplishing anything? We spend lots of energy carrying all that plastic for the sake of convenience. However, would it not be best if one card (yes one!) would pay for everything, discount everything, and reward all of our own personal consumer behaviors?

Last night my husband and I went to see a movie. Afterward, with our frequent diner cards in hand, we went to a sandwich shop. Upon presenting our fully filled-out cards for "one free sandwich," the young waiter nonchalantly responded, "sorry folks, this promotion expired last week."

Don't be silly dear, the more the merrier.
No, I'm fine, everything is done. I don't need any help at all.
You look tired, sit down.

# WHO'S COMING TO DINNER?

The holidays are almost upon us, and families are planning their annual dinners. Mom is making plans to include the whole family. She makes sure that everything looks festive. She'll drag out Grandma's pre-war dishes to grace the table. The chips on the plates appear larger than the portions of food served on them.

She spends many weeks baking cookies and freezing goodies for everyone to enjoy. Mom always fixes the main dish. She brings out her juicy turkey slathered with sauce and spices.

Mom will make sure to invite every member of the family, which has grown faster than the ears of corn on Grandpa's farm. She is known as the peacemaker in the family, always making sure no one gets their feelings hurt. One of the first things Mom does is make her list of who brings what food group. She is hoping that some of the relatives will help with the cooking and bring their special recipes—strange as they may be.

Who can forget last year's holiday events when the family got together? Aunt Minnie brought her unidentified cider something in a jug, which kept her tipsy for several days. Uncle Lester and Aunt Lena, who live far away, always bring their nine children and three dogs. Last year those kids held Grandma and Grandpa hostage until Grandma showed everyone how her dentures slide in and out of her mouth and Grandpa showed how his hairpiece came off. Unfortunately, one of the dogs got a hold of the thing and ran off with it.

What will Cousin Harley donate this time? He always surprises everybody when he brings wine from an unknown origin. Let's hope the two old spinsters of the clan won't bring their

# One Size Fits Most

homemade marinated mystery meat. Everyone who ate the stuff suffered severe cramps last time.

Auntie Zelda always brings her spiked fruit sap mixed with her homegrown tomato sauce. Last year she swore it helped her chickens lay much bigger eggs. She claims it gave her Russian sheep a thicker layer of wool.

Many relatives stayed at Mom's house last year. Which one will spread the gossip this time? We know this will happen again. Having houseguests means cleaning the extra rooms and bringing out the blankets that have been packed in mothballs. There is only so much room and so little time. But, Mom will manage to prepare for the extra company.

Mom has worked hard finishing all the cleaning, cooking, and baking, but all the hard work will pay off when we are all together again.

Of course, some of the family members need special menu variations. Aunt Zelda can't digest turkey very well, so last year we stuffed her portions in the blender and mixed it with her sweet potatoes. She thought it was the best sweet potatoes she'd ever tasted. Uncle Lester has an allergy to cranberry sauce that makes his face break out in hives. Grandma still has difficulty hanging on to her new dentures—we'll have her stick to mashed potatoes, cranberry sauce, and Aunt Zelda's sweet potato shake.

When the family and the holiday finally arrive, Mom is ready. The time flew and almost everybody had fun trading gossip and insults. Some events didn't go as planned. Uncle Harry lost his gold tooth in the gravy bowl while he was ladling some over his turkey. Uncle Gertin received the Heimlich maneuver after he tried to choke down two turkey legs at once. (He was showing off again for the nieces and nephews.) Thankfully, no one got sick on anybody's homemade concoction this year.

When everyone has finally gone home, Mom wonders if she should be the one to have the family holiday gathering next year. The problem is, no one else ever offers to do it.

Oh well, Mom will volunteer again for next year—just as usual.

# CHARGE IT

Every time I open my mail I'm bombarded with credit card offers. It's amazing how easy it is to obtain a credit card these days. Many credit card companies promise a low interest rate, easy monthly payments, and bonus points. It sounds like a great deal when the letter says "you're approved, no payment for three months."

But did you bother to read the fine print? Credit card companies assure us that using their card will give us peace of mind. But when the bills pile up I may lose my mind trying to make the payments.

Too bad credit cards don't come with warning instructions to let me know that when I bought that pair of $30 jeans on sale, I'd be paying for them for the next five years.

I use a credit card when I pump gas, or when I shop on the Net. When I go to a store and they refuse to take a personal check, I use my credit card. Who carries cash around these days? Buying groceries on credit saves time, but when the bill comes in the following month you're paying for food that has been consumed weeks ago.

Credit cards are not really a pal, and they may come back to haunt you for months, or even years to come. How often do I walk into a store and the nice clerk offers me instant credit? All I have to do is write down my address and phone number. Minutes later I have buying power.

My newly established credit is a piece of paper with a temporary number posing as my fairy godmother. It says that I may spend up to $1,000. Now I can take advantage of the "one day only" fabulous sale the store is having. However, there are other credit card charges waiting to be paid off. My other cards are charged to the

# One Size Fits Most

max, but I remember the promise of low interest and no payments for 90 days, so I think I have nothing to worry about. Having one more credit card can't hurt.

I spot a beautiful little holiday dress in my size, and there is no money left in my checking account. What am I going to do? I do have a brand-new line of credit. I have to make a decision—buy the dress of my dreams, or let someone else get their grubby hands on it? The nice clerk flashes a toothy smile encouragingly, as she swears up and down this dress is me! Not wanting to be a scrooge for the holidays, I figure, why not?

During the holidays most people spend more money. Buying Christmas presents for family and friends is important. Having a few extra credit cards at my disposal makes me feel like everything is free!

But suddenly, the holidays are over and my shopping spree has come to a screeching halt. The postman becomes my enemy as he smiles when he hands me a growing pile of credit card bills. The nice little clerks who offered me those little perks won't pay for my over-extended credit. There are no elves looking over my statements offering to help out. There's no tooth fairy to leave money under my pillow.

It was fun buying gifts for everyone while I was in the holiday spirit. I even added my grumpy supervisor's name to my gift list this year.

Here it is January, and I'm up to my kneecaps in debt. Eventually, the bills must be paid and when I am hit with a late charge for every credit card it will cost me dearly. It is in the credit card company's interest to charge a late fee. In fact, they're wishing people will just make the minimum payment. I'll be staring at these statements for sometime and I wonder if I'm ever going to use a credit card again.

Stores will continue having promotions for new customers hoping they will open a charge account with them. But I may want to do some thinking before I accept another credit card offer, if I don't want to make payments throughout the next year for last year's purchases.

# POST NASAL DRIP SYNDROME

Do you know what it feels like to wake up thinking someone is holding a pillow over your face? Then you realize that your schnozz is just plugged up.

Oh, oh, I've got a cold. Who is the culprit who donated this miserable disease to me? Most likely it is from my loved ones who always share their germs only with their mom. They probably inherited the "bug" from one of their pals.

My head is pounding, and the backs of my eyeballs feel like burning cinders. My kneecaps ache, I feel so rotten. Every time I inhale, my chest feels as if I'm sucking up the steam from a hot air balloon. But, I've got to get up and wait on the family. The show must go on. They're certainly not going to wait on me. God forbid I should have a sniffle.

When I walk into the kitchen, the kids and hubby are staring at my poor puffed-up eyes and red nose. They wonder—how could Mom have a cold? She can't be sick. Not our mom! The darlings are waiting for their cereal and milk. They couldn't possibly get up and get their own food.

I have committed the ultimate sin. How dare Mom get sick!

When they have finally left the house for the day, I decide I should try some of the cold medicine that is stored in the cabinet. I reach for the cold-plus-rest medicine and sniff, I wonder how I could ever have made the kids take the stuff. After reading the instructions on the labels, I'm convinced the makers of the foul-smelling product are trying to reduce the population.

After finally uncovering the meaning of all the ingredients in

# One Size Fits Most

the container and deciphering the codes, which couldn't possibly be written in English, I now know what it says. *"Don't drive or operate any machinery, Don't drink any alcohol, Do not use if taking blood pressure medicine, Do not take if pregnant, Take only with food.* (Who can eat?) By the time I've read all the dos and don'ts, I had better oblige or this stuff is going to kill me. (I'd just as soon die a natural death!)

I decide to lie down and try to get some rest. By the time the kids get home I'm really feeling lousy. They're surprised I'm not better yet! The color and shapes of the cold sores on my lips resemble the rust spots on a car. I've rubbed so much Vaseline under my sore nose that when I try to blow it, I have a heck of a time keeping the hanky from sliding.

While the kids whine about doing their chores, I muster up the strength to call the doctor. He suggests, "Take some aspirin and go to bed." (Where have you heard that phrase before?) He also tells me to slow down and take it easy. (Is he kidding?) Does he think Alice from the "Brady Bunch" lives in my house, and Mike Brady is my understanding husband?

When hubby gets home, he tells me how tired I look! Just the thing I've been dying to hear. He offers to help with dinner, and calls out for pizza. The thought of food sends chills up and down my spine. The kids promise that if I go to bed, they will be very quiet. Gratefully, I take them up on the offer. Crawling back into bed makes me feel guilty, though. As sick as I am, I think of all the things I have to do. Finally I doze off.

The next morning, I'm actually feeling better. When I tell the children that I'm feeling better today, they are so relieved that they show their gratitude by dumping all their problems that they wanted to share yesterday, on me. Oh boy, I want to run back to the bedroom—I'm not feeling that well after all.

Well, I reason wearily—this is business as usual.

# VALENTINE'S DAY

Valentine's Day is coming up, and of course, we'll have to go along with tradition.

We expect our sweethearts to buy us presents that include candy and sexy lingerie, to prove how much they love us.

Today, a Valentine card costs at least a couple of bucks; that is, if you want to buy a cheap card. You can also create a card with your own words, but it costs five or six bucks!

I remember when the kids were little we would buy those little candy hearts for their school chums. We'd stuff the candy hearts into small envelopes. The candy spoke for itself—it read: "Be My Valentine." Now, that was easy, and if the teacher was well-liked, there was a little something for him or her, too.

Women love to make their hubbies feel guilty if they don't show how much they care for their "little women." Never mind that the rest of the year he is working his buns off to put food on the table. Why is it, if—God forbid—hubby doesn't bring home five pounds of tooth-decaying chocolate, we are so unhappy? Maybe he'll take you out to dinner at your favorite restaurant. We do know that many holidays are money-making times for stores and restaurants—still we expect goodies, trinkets, and meals out.

I remember when I was carrying our first child, hubby had to go out of town for a day. He spent hours working hard and traveled miles to get home. On his way he passed a small cheese shop in Wisconsin. He stopped and purchased several imported cheeses. When he arrived home he told me to close my eyes and hold out my hands. I felt something heavy and squealed with joy!

## One Size Fits Most

Having been raised in Amsterdam, Holland, an Edam cheese was probably the most loving Valentine gift he could have ever given me. It didn't look anything like a heart, but the wrapper around the cheese *was* red.

Now it was my turn to show him how much I loved him. Oops, I guess I forgot his gift. With all my concern about receiving MY Valentine gift that showed his love, I honestly forgot all about HIS present. I thought desperately of something to do. I found an old Valentine card and presented this to him—hopefully he wouldn't remember I had given him this same card last year. I consider this my contribution to recycling paper.

This year I'll make sure I get a head start. I'll show him how much I love him by digging out the candles and cooking his favorite meal. Then I'll spare him the hassle of having to go shopping for my Valentine. I'll do the shopping for something I really want, wrap it up, and be sure to thank him during our lovely dinner—for the lovely gift I bought myself, from him, for Valentine's Day.

# COOKING WITH FLAVOR AND STYLE

Do you remember the first time you cooked a meal for your loved one? Did he tell you that he really enjoyed the dinner you fixed for him? (Though he wondered what the shriveled, blackened thing on his plate was.) After a severe bout with heartburn and a large dose of antacid, you realized your cooking skills needed improvement.

Cooking has never been my favorite pastime. Even with today's easy and quick-fix tips, I still manage to mess up a meal. I've tried experimenting with new recipes, but many failed the taste test. My future in cooking looked grim. Evidence showed that eating food in my kitchen was hazardous to the stomach. Even our dog, Hercules, was put on beano® after eating the leftover scraps every day.

My family survived the early years after many trials and tribulations—and enormous amounts of antacids. I followed experts Julia Child and the Galloping Gourmet on TV in the hope that my cooking might improve.

Most of the dishes created by celebrity cooks didn't appeal to the kids. So, when I served my family a meal, the kitchen usually cleared out fast. We armed the fridge with frozen dinners and stocked the cabinets with lots of canned goods. We also kept Pizza Hut's phone number close at hand.

A neighbor shared her recipe for all-day stew. It was created by throwing the ingredients together early in the morning and putting it in the oven for the rest of the day. This recipe worked for a while until the family finally refused to eat the stuff. Hercules opted for the neighbor's scraps until I changed our menu.

# One Size Fits Most

When we got our first microwave oven there was reason to believe my cooking would improve. Friends suggested a course in microwave cooking. I gained some experience during the cooking course, and extra pounds sampling the goodies.

Finally, when I felt confident that my cooking had passed the test among the family, we joined a small gourmet dinner group in our town. We invited some friends for our first gourmet dinner, and those who weren't afraid to eat my food showed up. What a relief it was, when not one person got sick afterward. I also found out that not all good cooks are perfect. At a friend's dinner party we had just sat down to a wonderful meal cooked by our hostess, who had tried out one of her new microwave recipes. Everything went great until a loud "boom" from her kitchen startled the guests.

There had been an explosion in the microwave. Our hostess had attempted to cook eggs in her new microwave oven. Unfortunately, the eggs were still in the shell. She had forgotten to pierce the eggshells before putting them in the microwave.

With all the fancy cookbooks and timesaving recipes, fixing a meal is a lot easier than it used to be. But what if you can't find all the ingredients you need? When you look at pictures of a scrumptious meal that takes very little time to fix, you want to get out your pots and pans and toss it together. But if you just got home from a long day at work, and you don't have all the ingredients on hand, do you want to go to the store just for one item? Some recipes say that you can substitute one spice for another. But the meal may not taste the same when you use different spices. Also, there are some ingredients that are virtually impossible to find.

How often do you find yourself running through all the local grocery stores searching the shelves for one ingredient? By the time you have collected all those spices, your family may not like the meal and you'll probably never use them again! You'll end up having your shelves and cupboards filled with unused jars and cans of spices.

When there are just the two of you, after the kids have finally left home, you face another problem. Now you have to learn how to make dinner for two. How can you follow a recipe for two? Cut everything in half? What if the recipe calls for three and one-quarter cups of flour? You'll need a calculator just to do the math.

Maybe you should stop by the bookstore and pick up a *Cooking For 2* cookbook.

Or, maybe you should take the night off and visit a fine restaurant. Hercules will certainly enjoy the leftovers.

# One Size Fits Most

# COMMERCIAL
# BURNOUT

Aren't there days when every little noise drives you nuts? Every day, people are subjected to all kinds of loud noises. Especially when facing a long and hectic day, or when I'm trying to make my way to work. Cars are blasting rowdy tunes, and the ear-piercing screech of tires can be heard throughout the cities. Suddenly I hear the roaring of sirens from police cars buzzing past me. Ambulances zoom by at a neck-breaking speed, causing me to scurry over to the side of the road. My day has just begun.

At the workplace, all day long, I'm inundated with demands. I spend a great deal of the day listening to ringing phones and running from one place to another, getting through the day meeting all the deadlines. It makes my head spin and I'm ready to go home and get some rest from all this mayhem.

When at last I stumble toward my car you'd think the day is over. Think again! I slide my exhausted body behind the wheel and turn on the radio to catch the latest news. The first thing that hits my ears is dozens of commercials blaring at me about how to relax and how to rid myself of a pounding headache. Quickly I switch to another station, but someone is peddling TUMS® for an upset stomach. For the next fifteen minutes I am blasted by one commercial after another. The only way to get rid of my migraine is to shut off the radio! All I want is some soft, gentle music to soothe my tired, achy head.

Before rushing home I have to make a quick stop at the grocery store to pick up a few items for dinner. The store is packed with people by the time I get there. After the hustle and bustle

# One Size Fits Most

of digging and shoving my way through the battlefield of aisles, I'm ready to flee from this madhouse.

Once back in the car I am confronted with yet another battle. This involves making it through the war zone of traffic lights and their random stops.

At last I've made it home. I'm just in time to chill out, change into something comfortable, throw the food in the microwave, and turn on the TV. There are just minutes left to catch the news before the family bursts in, making their demands on me. I hunt through the channels but all I'm getting is another overdose of commercials. There are so many of them the news will be history when I finally hear about it.

Commercials are designed to get peoples' attention. Yes, some are funny, but many are extremely obnoxious. How can I relax when I hear a commercial with telephones ringing, babies crying, dogs barking, and rock bands slamming their tunes while I watch? It drowns out the message they're trying to convey to the listeners.

Commercials are necessary. They pay for the programs. But less noise and a little peace and quiet after a long day works wonders. When I want to relax, I hate to listen to those head-banging, mind-numbing commercials, the best thing to do is turn off the tube, lose the squawk box, take a couple of aspirin, grab a good book or a newspaper, and catch up on some reading.

# WEDDING GIFTS

**WARNING:**
**FUTURE**
**GARAGE SALE**
**ITEM INSIDE**

Spring and summer are a busy time for weddings, so it was no surprise when my hairstylist informed me that she was planning her nuptials. I asked her where she had registered for her bridal showers. She said that she had registered at several major department stores. The trouble was, she had received many duplicate gifts, and she didn't want to hurt people's feelings by returning the gifts she didn't want. Especially those gifts from family and close friends.

She also discovered that some gifts did not come in the original boxes, and she had no way of knowing where these gifts were purchased. She had to wonder if some of the items were used, washed, and boxed up. It would be nice if she could return the items for cash, although some stores refuse to give a cash refund and instead offer a voucher.

I didn't think to register for my wedding. We ended up with several identical toasters, four coffeepots, and four boxes of juice glasses that matched nothing we owned. Years later when we moved, I still had those same juice glasses in the basement. We had an October wedding, so the tie-dye bedsheets we received made great Halloween outfits that year.

When a couple plans their wedding, they carefully choose the patterns for their dishes, linens, and accessories. Newlyweds often need just about everything for their home, and they want to decorate and choose stuff that is to their taste. The bride doesn't want to keep her future spouse's old chipped and cracked dinner service from his bachelor days, or inherit Aunt Minnie's ancient sewing machine. She wants to fill their home with new things, and decorate in her own style.

Unfortunately, not all guests think about the wishes of the bride and groom, and the newlyweds may end up with a bunch of unwanted gifts. It would be great if people would check the bridal registry at a store before they purchase a gift, and then remember to check it off the registry computer.

When my sister got married she didn't want to sound ungrateful when our favorite cousin gave her a set of serving bowls that had been in the family for years. The shape and colors looked so ridiculous her two pets refused to eat and drink from the bowls. When our cousin comes to visit, my sister always makes sure that the ugly heirlooms are on display. I still bring out Aunt Tilly's ceramic fruit plates from the attic when she comes on her annual visits. She had made several identical sets for all her nieces.

I remember when someone gifted us with a crockpot on our wedding day. Since we already had two, I decided to return the extra crockpot. With the name of the store on one of the boxes, I decided to take that one back. Upon returning the crockpot to the store, I was told that this particular one had been a promotional gift with the purchase of a dishwasher more than three years ago.

If you don't have time to shop for a wedding present, a gift certificate or a check might be the solution. Couples can always use cash. A monetary gift is also better because most couples take a vacation immediately following the wedding. My check has never been refused by anyone, and I don't have to go shopping. It makes it easier for the newlyweds to send you a thank you note when you give a check, because there's no confusion as to who sent the gift!

# BEATING THE CROWD

Remember when shopping at a grocery store was so simple? Today, going to the local grocery store is like visiting Disneyland. You don't know where anything is.

Even the people who work at the store are confused as to where the items are located. Just when you've spent half of your day getting re-acquainted with the store shelves, someone re-arranges everything. Now, you've got to start all over. I wonder if the store management decides to hold weekly drills to keep the working folks in shape. Aisle 1-5 used to house canned soups and assorted crackers. They now have been replaced with salad dressing, olives, and pickles. Or was it tuna and Spam™? Who can remember?

I find myself racing through the store trying to remember where the needed foods are. Many people have little time to spend in a grocery store. They would like to buzz in and out, but they exhaust the little energy they've got left trying to find something for the evening meal.

Finally, after having finished playing games looking for stuff and wondering "Where's the beef?" I hurry to the checkout counter. I feel rushed, and hope to beat the crowd. What has happened? The store didn't look this busy when I first got here. Does everyone come to shop at the same time?

The sign above the grocery counter reads: "10 items or less and cash only." (Sure, I always carry a ton of cash around.) So, I move on to the next checkout line. Again, there is a sign telling me "15 items or less." What? Do they expect me to count every food item? How in the world does anyone have time to go home and cook the stuff when you spend half the evening searching for and counting the groceries? Do they expect the customer to do all that? Whatever happened to good service?

The lady in front of me has now unloaded her basket, thirty items later she smiles apologetically and says, "I didn't see the sign." Is she blind? The sign is larger than the checkout counter, and she missed it! She fumbles for her checkbook, holding eight people hostage. All the while I'm trying to be patient and keep my cool. Goody, she has finally located her checkbook. Oops, no more checks left. Great! She finds her credit card. She puffs in relief, as if she has done the world a favor.

Meanwhile, the ice cream my hubby so loves is starting to melt. The frozen burritos I wanted to use for the weekend should be kept frozen until you microwave them. Fifteen minutes, and now, seven frustrated people later, it is my turn to check out my thawed-out food. I push my cart with only a few items to a cranky checkout person. She growls, "Do you have a saving's card?" I honestly forgot to pull the thing out of my wallet. With all the shuffling and rushing around, I forgot to check. After I've retrieved the saving's card, it's my turn to look apologetic.

The people behind me now give ME the evil eye. The clerk throws the food to the packer, and he asks, "Paper or plastic?" I mumble my preference, as long as she hurries me through the checkout. As she checks out my purchases she asks me the prices on the items. How am I supposed to know the price on an item? The groceries aren't marked except with a code, but the machine doesn't seem to catch the code. The clerk hollers loudly, "Price check on Gyne-Lotrimin!" I now want to crawl into a hole. I hope the grouchy-looking man behind me never heard of the stuff. At last the groceries are bagged and loaded into the car. I'm on my way.

Feeling pooped, I'm glad to get home just in time to fix dinner. Good grief! Suddenly I realize that through all the struggle to get my groceries, I've forgotten to buy the most important ingredient for the meal. Uh oh, hubby's home! Quickly, I dial Pizza Hut®.

# ALL
# THUMBS

Here in my corner of the world, we're surrounded by the beauty of trees and lots of flowering gardens. Each year, people give much of their time and devotion planting new seeds, and taking an interest in beautifying their homes inside and out with greenery.

While cruising through town, I notice some of the prettiest and well-maintained parks. It has been said it takes a lot of patience, a green thumb, and a lot of love to care for flowers and plants.

There are people who have the talent to care for plants and the perseverance to nurture their gardens. There are also those of us who are all thumbs, like me. When friends come to visit, I rush to the nearest flower store and replace every sickly-looking plant in the house.

Try as I may, I have never been able to keep a houseplant alive for longer than a few weeks. If not for my husband's love for nature, my plants wouldn't make it through the night. Whenever I forgot to water my plants and they had that droopy look, my husband came to their aid and put them on life support. He'd nurture almost every plant back to health. He has also rescued plants that I had accidentally drowned. When my hubby was out of town, the plants feared for their lives. I couldn't help feeling envy when I looked at our neighbors' yards. I have tried talking to my plants and playing soft music, but usually my plants go into shock and keel over in misery. I have read stacks of books on how to care for living plants and I've tried every gimmick, including adding loads of nutrients and stroking them as you would a pet.

# One Size Fits Most

Recently, we purchased several lovely hibiscus trees. I was happy with my choice, and was told that if I followed the directions, my trees would last for years. The pamphlet that had been included stated that the trees needed bright sunlight, indoors or outdoors, and water every few days. Two weeks later, the poor things went into shock. The once lovely trees had been stripped of their beauty, and though my husband tried to revive them, they suffered a slow death. I decided that I would never buy another living plant.

When my birthday arrived, I received several arrangements of plants and flowers from my family and friends. I was delighted and vowed they would live until my next birthday. To my dismay, the plants didn't even survive till Mother's Day. Someone suggested that I invest in artificial flower arrangements and plants. Having been raised in Amsterdam, Holland, where tulip festivals and flower shows are the norm, fake flowers just didn't seem right. But given the fact that I didn't have a green thumb, I decided to give the impostors a try.

I shopped through many flower shops and nurseries looking for a "real fake." At one retail store, I had to make several trips and some of the workers began to know me by the tall, oversized silk plants riding in a cart throughout the store. Transporting my new friends home in my car was an experience in and of itself. My friends and neighbors began to ask about my newfound chemistry with foliage.

In fact, I discovered the plants cleaned up a lot easier than the living ones and also seemed less appetizing to our children and pets. When I got tired of the colors I hid them in a closet.

As far as working with flowers in our garden, I leave that up the man of the house—and Mother Nature.

# WHO ME... DIET?

The holidays are just around the corner. TV ads are flashing lovely creatures in fancy evening wear, showing off their glorious shapes. Stores are loading up on halter dresses and skimpy, tight-fitting pantsuits.

Out are pyramid tent dresses and fluffy clown pants that hid last year's bulges. In are tiny minis and teeny micros forcing us to keep our tummies sucked in.

I go to work to rid myself of those dreaded ten pounds of weight that have dared to sneak up on my unsuspecting body. Shamelessly, those pounds are peeping out of my clothing making me feel oh, so guilty.

Didn't I look just great at the last Christmas party? There was so little warning. No one said, "Hey! The pounds are coming, so watch it!" I only ate a few hors d'oeuvres at most parties—so what if I munched down that last cheese puff? It was just sitting there calling my name. Then there was the sweet chocolate heart my hubby gave me for Valentine's Day. How could I refuse it? And, God forbid, he mustn't eat it—Doc told him to watch his cholesterol and high blood pressure.

All right, from now until Thanksgiving I'll sweat and starve. I'll jog (and get shinsplints), eat tuna (ugh!), and bruise my backside doing thousands of sit-ups. I'll join a gym.

It sounded great at first, but after ten minutes of all this hard work, try walking to the water fountain. Muscles that I never knew existed caused me to walk like a pregnant woman. Well, what do I expect? My dormant muscles haven't been out of their cages for years.

# One Size Fits Most

I've finally had enough of the too-tight clothes, zero willpower, and fat jokes! So I race over to the fitness center. Once there I notice the skinny people who must have been working out for years, and I wonder how long I'm going to last competing with these slinky-looking women

I will force myself to work harder to get into shape. I'm huffing and puffing and sweating off the unflattering pounds, all the while praying desperately for some super-human strength to be able to live through my first exercise regimen.

Suddenly fat foods have become a no-no. I'm learning to combine exercise, nutritious food, and a healthy sleeping pattern instead of sneaking off to the kitchen during the night in search of last night's leftovers.

Move over Cindy Crawford! Something is happening. I no longer need panty hose that say "Queen Size, Control Top, Extra Snug." No more lying flat on my back to zip up my blue jeans. Friends start to tell me how slim I look. "It's nothing," I reply nonchalantly. "I never worry about my weight." (I lie.)

Hubby is impressed and wants to buy me a jumbo banana split to celebrate. (Is he kidding? After dieting myself to nearly comatose?) Now that I've worked so hard I can enjoy the latest in micro and mini fashions, even if only for a little while. Eventually, those five pounds will sneak back and attach themselves to my hips and thighs if I dare sneak the dessert I love. I will struggle to keep that from happening, and vow to go back to working out at the fitness center. But for now—I'm enjoying myself by saying, "Who me? I never worry about my weight!"

# WHO KNOWS HOSE?

When was the last time you purchased a pair of panty hose and felt comfortable when you put them on? After several hours of wearing hose, do you ever wish you didn't have to wear them again? It is said that you are not dressed up unless you are wearing panty hose. So why is it so hard to find a pair that is easy to slip in to and out of?

A pair of panty hose should last more than just one day. How often are you ready to leave the house and suddenly you notice that you have a run? You're getting ready to go to work, and rush your way into your panty hose, and boom! You've ripped them to pieces. Of course, you're fresh out. Your hose didn't last like it said it would. Every pair you put on this week had snagged before you left your house.

I have shopped the world over in search of a pair of panty hose that would give me a comfortable fit, and make me look ten pounds lighter. I also hoped I could find some that would last me at least one day. So far I've had no luck.

Where can a person find a pair of panty hose that fits like a glove, wears like second skin, and doesn't feel like you are being strangled? Wouldn't you just like to own one pair that doesn't cut off your blood supply after wearing them a couple of hours? It couldn't possibly have been a woman who designed the spandex contraption. She would have mercy on women.

When you buy a pair of panty hose that says size "medium-large", and the chart on the package says they fit women 4'10" and 125-150 pounds. They must be joking. These polyester hip and thigh crunchers wouldn't fit a child.

# One Size Fits Most

After you've tried on the queen- and jumbo-sized hose, you begin to suspect that companies must have had model Kate Moss in mind when they designed them. Can you picture Kate Moss and attorney general Janet Reno both trying to fit into a pair of hose that says "one size fits all"?

Lots of panty hose have a control top to help suck in the tummy bulge. What happens to the extra overflow? The last time I bought a pair, the sticker on the package said "queen size, extra long." As I struggled my way into them, the crotch barely reached my kneecaps. When I finally managed to worm the rest of my body in I knew I had been punished.

Now, I am by no means skinny, but neither am I a heavy person. I barely hit 5 feet in height and weigh about 125 pounds, or is it 135 pounds? Who's counting? If you ever find a pair of hose that do fit, handle them with care. You never want to be in a hurry wiggling in and out of them when going to the ladies' room. Try joining your dinner guest after getting your hose stuck in the zipper in the back of your jump suit.

Also, watch out if you have long nails. They can rip your hose to shreds.

Much of the same happens when you buy knee-highs. If you buy a package with several pair, you hope they are well made and have a wide band. The so-called wide band is so tight by the day's end your ankles resemble those of a pregnant woman.

The stores carry all kinds of panty hose, so you'd think you could find some that are made to fit your shape. There are panty hose with reinforced toes. How many times have you put your toe right through your hose?

Years ago women wore stockings and hooked them up to a garter belt. At least you didn't have to hike your stockings over your hips and force your entire body into them. Going to the ladies' room was also easier. When you got a run in one of your stockings you could always carry a spare one in your purse. Have you ever carried an extra set of panty hose in a small evening bag?

I really envy men. They just throw on a pair of socks and when they get a hole, or a run, in them no one can tell. The man is ready to go even when his socks don't match. I could borrow my hubby's over-the-calf socks when I wear a long skirt. Or, I could wait for some designer to produce a line of king-sized panty hose with room to spare.

But until that time comes women will have to suffer by pushing, pulling, and stretching their bodies into spandex and Lycra.

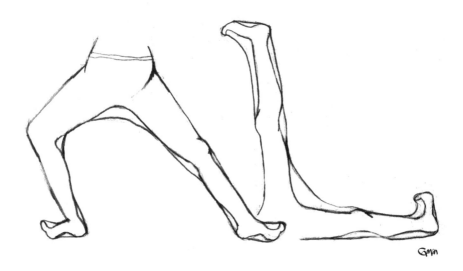

**EARLY BIRD SPECIALS
4 PM TO 6 PM
SENIOR CITIZEN'S
DISCOUNT**

# WELL, AT LEAST YOU GET A DISCOUNT

Life begins at fifty!

Hubby says, "Honey, you look as good as the day I met you." That's about twenty years (and pounds) ago! Friends say, "Welcome to menopause, arthritis, and Geritol®!"

My children's friends tell me they sure hope they'll look like me when they get to be my age. Gee thanks, I guess.

My recent check-up reveals high cholesterol and high blood pressure. The doctor tells me that I could use some calcium for my teeth and bones. The dentist gave me a tube of Polygrip® after he readjusted my partial plate.

And aren't grandchildren wonderful! After my three-year-old grandchild looked at my face for a while, she said, "Grandma, you have stripes on your face." I told her that "those stripes belong on Grandma's face. Grandma has earned those stripes." Now I'm just waiting for my stars!

I went to the mall for some serious shopping. The young clerks are so great looking, dressed in the cute little miniskirts and sexy sweaters. I picked up a miniskirt and talked myself into trying it on. Why? I have no idea. My hips have been utterly rearranged! My waist almost matches them, and my kneecaps look like boulders—and those thighs—ugh, hard to tell where they start and stop! Talk about tree trunks! My legs looked awful!

I don't have that "sweater look" any more. Maybe a new brassiere would help—the kind that is long and covers up the tummy part. All right, I'll go try it on. It feels and looks like an orthopedic jumpsuit! The so-called slimming brassiere pushes everything down instead of up. Now everything is pushed below

One Size Fits Most

the hips, and I look like I'm carrying an oversized set of saddle-bags!

I feel defeated as I climb back into my big old jeans and sweat shirt. It's just another fad, anyway. Just not my style. Off to the local ice-cream shop!

The young thing behind the counter cheerfully informs me that I'm entitled to a senior citizen's discount. Just what I needed to hear! But she asked so nicely, I can't refuse. After all—a penny saved is a penny earned.

Suddenly a thought occurs to me while I'm enjoying my ice cream. How about some new makeup? Maybe it will cover up those "stripes" on my face. I've read those magazines that talk about products that take ten to fifteen years off your face.

At the makeup shop a young lady pulls out a huge chart. She sells me enough night cream to grease up a hockey field and enough anti-wrinkle cream to smooth out the Black Hills of South Dakota.

Next comes the hair color. I've been plucking out gray hairs for the past five years, so it must be time for a change in color. I remember when my mother used to put shoe polish on her roots! Maybe I could look like those gals on the TV soaps. After all, most of them are in their forties and fifties.

On returning home I sneak into the bathroom and go to work. I read all the directions carefully, and wonder who has time to spend on all this stuff. Finally, seven hours and $80 later, I come out of the bathroom just in time. Hubby is home. I meet him at the door in a slinky robe and greet him in a husky voice, hand-ing him a drink. He asks, "Are you all right?" He wonders if I've had a drink or two myself.

As I ask him about his day, he really starts to worry. All the while I am waiting for that "magic moment" when he really notices me.

He asks, "What's for dinner, Hon?" He sits down and devours his food, shaking his head at all the bad news on TV and whistling at all the young, sexy-looking women in the commer-cials. By dessert time I'm really starting to wonder why he hasn't noticed my "improved looks." As he gets up from the table and pops into his favorite chair by the TV, I burst into tears. "What's wrong, honey? Dinner and dessert were great."

I tearfully tell him all I went through just to look younger for him. He puts his arms around me and says, "You're already beautiful to me. That's why I didn't notice any change. I married you for love."

I explain how I was feeling "old," and that I wanted to make him happy. He says he never noticed my graying hair, sagging bosom, or wrinkles.

He says, "Look at me! I feel great just the way I am." Even though he has gained at least four pant sizes. He enjoys people telling him that his gray hair gives him a "distinguished look"— or that bald is beautiful.

Being over fifty isn't all bad! With a little help from Doan's® pills, BENGAY®, Geritol®, and Polygrip® you can actually enjoy life!

SO, WHAT WAS WRONG WITH THE OLD ONE?

# NEW AND IMPROVED

Recently I did some shopping at one of my favorite gift shops and as I walked inside I discovered I was in the wrong place— or so I thought. The shop had a new owner and different merchandise. The previous owners had relocated across the street because they needed more room for the new and improved products.

Some things need change and improvements for good reasons. However, sometimes the "old" is better. We are constantly subjected to changes whether we like it or not. When was the last time you walked into the grocery store and your favorite food had been replaced by a new and improved product? I discovered that my snack bar had been replaced. My taste buds were perfectly happy with the way my snack bar tasted before. How dare they change the ingredients in the snack bar I loved!

I made a mad dash to every grocery store in the area and purchased all the old boxes of my snack bars. I wrote a letter and pleaded my case with the company in the hope that they might restore the taste of my old snack bars. A marriage reconciliation between Ivana and Donald Trump would have had a much better chance. In answer to my letter, I received a taped telephone message from the company explaining that their snack bars had been upgraded and provided with 15 essential vitamins and minerals, more calcium, more natural fibers, less cholesterol, and fewer calories. Did I care about these ingredients? If I wanted a vitamin, I would take a vitamin!

Just when we get used to an item we like, companies decide it needs to be new and improved. How many times can something

# One Size Fits Most

be improved?

On a recent trip to the grocery store, I wanted to pick up a few cans of vegetable soup for lunch. I had been using the same soup for my family for many years. But the store had replaced the vegetable soup with new and improved cans of vegetable soup. I decided to give it a try. What could they do to vegetable soup? What a disappointment! This soup didn't taste the same. Once again, I wrote to the company. They apologized and sent us a whole case of their new and improved vegetable soup.

Companies are always advertising, knowing that people will buy their latest products. Does this mean the stuff in my cupboards and closets is not that great?

For years we enjoyed the flavor of a "brand-new" toothpaste. The stuff worked great and it was highly recommended by "4 out of 5 dentists." Soon the tube of toothpaste had decreased in size and good flavor, but the price didn't!

I discovered we have drawers and closets bulging with products that have been new and improved. People buy the products every time something new and improved comes on the market. We run out and purchase those items hoping we are getting something just a little better. Companies that advertise their products are doing exactly what they set out to do. They keep improving their products and we approve by buying them. The "new and improved" products give us a reason to tuck away the old and bring in the new.

Just when we had figured out how easily we are drawn to new products, I spotted a new refrigerator with lots of "new and improved" options. The one we have is a bit out of date and the new color matches my new oven and microwave. It also has a new and improved ice maker...

# ALL IN A DAY'S WORK

How often did your mother tell you that *cleanliness is next to godliness?* She probably also told you that *a clean house is a happy house.* So, remembering these words—to work we go—scrubbing and scraping plastered-on dirt from the house. From dawn to dusk we work until we are totally exhausted by the end of the day.

At last we tuck away the "mean, cleaning, sucking machine," and we enter the next phase of our tasks. What to fix for dinner. The family has devoured so much fish and chicken their bodies should start developing scales and feathers. I want to fix something easy and nutritious to please my loved ones.

I do a quick search for a simple recipe. Then I happen to come across one of Aunt Martha's prehistoric recipe books. Scanning through the recipes, I wonder if stores still stock these pre-Betty Crocker ingredients. Time is wasting, I have to think fast. Liver and onions are for punishment only. Fish is out after I've spent hours cleaning the stove. They're tired of dogs and burgers on the grill. At last I locate an updated cookbook. Flipping through the pages, I find several palatable meals.

From a distance I hear familiar noises. "It can't be," I whisper in sheer panic. But alas, the kids are home from school. "Lord," I moan aloud, still sweating from the last load of laundry. Where has the time gone? I still haven't finished today's chores.

"We want our snack now, Mom," I hear the harmonious shouts. I open the cupboard and realize with the busy day I've had I didn't have time to go to the store and stock up on snacks. Quickly I think of something I can fix before the poor things starve. Popcorn, that will do. I dash around the kitchen to gather some goodies. Oh, no! There is no butter. Didn't I just buy butter?

"We have to hurry and get to practice," a demanding voice urges you on. Handing them each a banana I'm on the way escorting the royal party to their battlefields.

After chauffeuring the kids to their destinations I pick up the weekly groceries. I spend so much on food I could have taken the family on a three-day holiday.

Hubby just arrived home and wants a little appetizer and soda before dinner. Does he think he is on "Fantasy Island" and Mr. Roarke and his assistant Tattoo are there to greet him with delicacies? I toss him a couple of carrots to keep him from withering away and proceed with the evening meal.

Finally, the family sits down to eat the meal I, and my bag of miracles, produced. Everyone can relax and share stories instead of watching TV. But the food isn't to everyone's taste and crabbing and fussing becomes the evening's entertainment. I'm about ready to turn on the TV, but think better of it.

After everyone has eaten every bit of food from their plates, it is time to gather the clean-up committee. The younger members leap from the table, rushing off to do their homework. The male spouse of the house vows he will help me after his evening nap. Momentarily I close my eyes and drift off into a semi-conscious dream state visualizing elves helping me with the dishes. Suddenly my vision is shattered by a loved one who needs my help with homework.

I decide I'd better do the dishes and prepare for another day of cleaning, and scrubbing, and cooking. Then I remember more of my mother's words—*a woman's work is never done!* It's all in a day's work.

# NEED A HAND, ANYONE?

When we decided to do some remodeling on our house we never realized this would be a waiting game. Over the next few months we had meetings with several builders to work out an estimate for the project. Months later we were still waiting for the first guy to give us his estimate for the job.

We decided we wanted our sun porch insulated and baseboard heating units installed. But, unless your house has been stripped and torn down by a tornado, and needs to be completely rebuilt, don't call just any builder.

Some builders considered the remodeling job too small, unless it is a slow month—or a few rainy days pop up—they can't be bothered. Gee, isn't that thoughtful? The price tag sure isn't small!

By the time we were on our fifth contractor for an estimate, we still had few replies. Are some jobs just too small? Recently, we had our house painted, by what we thought would be a professional painter. It started out great. We hired a young man whose work was considered excellent by some people. He never told me that he would leave me, for personal reasons, with a half-painted house. I hate to tell you what the house looked like when he said he needed a rest. I wanted to put him to rest!

It was a good thing my husband made a grab for the paint can in my hands, because when I saw what the painter had done to the walls, I wanted to dump that paint on him. Figuring the size of the hospital bill might be a bit more costly than the rotten paint job, I reluctantly handed hubby the can.

The next few weeks were hell. We tried to find someone to finish what another person had messed up. But that's like digging

# One Size Fits Most

up the cement driveway. Four paint crews and a deflated bank account later, the job was finished. I was told that it was very difficult to match up the color that was already applied to the walls. The guy that I had dearly wanted to smack in the head with the paint (had my spouse not stopped me) had taken all the paint (that we had paid for).

I have learned never to pay more money down than necessary before the job is done. But being a softy, I had paid most of the money to the guy. He said he needed it. Guess an old dog can always be taught a few new tricks!

I can still tell where the paint was blended together. I suppose you could call it modern art. The rooms have that special "swirly" look. Picasso would have been proud.

We are considering doing some wallpapering. Of course, this means more estimates.

But there is no reason why one couldn't have some friends over to lend a helping hand—with some dinner and a promise to help them when they need it.

I can remember spending two days doing a tiny bathroom. My friend and I ate McDonald's, drank seven pots of coffee in one day, and told our husbands we were saving them money. My friend's husband still asks how his wife's helping could possibly save him money. I told him that by her helping me with my wallpaper, I would help them with their painting and wallpapering. Of course, my friend's house consisted mostly of paneling.

So every time you see these great friends that so kindly gave their time helping you do your wallpapering, you're going to wonder—are they going to ask me for help on their house? Might we have to baby-sit their pit bull while they're in Florida?

So, for the sake of friendship and peace of mind, call the professionals. With any luck and a lot of money, you may just find the right people to work on your home. Just ask for references and whatever you do—don't pay any more up front than is absolutely necessary.

So remember—stick with a professional to wallpaper. There really are a few good ones out there to do the job. You just have to search to find them. Need a plumber, anyone?

# ROMANTIC NOVELS AND SOAPS

A lot of people enjoy watching and following the lives of their favorite stars.

When you turn on your TV set, you wonder how these people can look so good and fresh. We all tend to envy the beautiful stars, especially the ones on our favorite soaps.

Those girls and guys look very glamorous and sexy. They're usually wealthy and wear fabulous clothes. You rarely see one of these women looking sloppy with her hair tucked in a bun or wearing a babushka while she's schlepping food to the table. Their fashionable clothes fit their slim, sculptured shapes to perfection, and their jewels are to die for. When did you ever see a soap character with her hair in curlers, packing her hubby's lunch bucket? I have yet to see these women change a diaper or stuff a load of laundry in the washing machine.

The men on the soaps have sexy bods, chiseled cheekbones, money to burn, and women to spare. They can't be faithful to just one woman for more than a few episodes.

They're in love, and out of love, faster than you can push the buttons on the remote control to another program. Most couples are married at least three or four times per season. They change partners more often than we change our bedsheets. If you miss a couple of episodes, you haven't missed much. Every few weeks you see your heroes split up with their lovers. He's found a NEW love and she's found an OLD one! When falling in love and marrying as many times as some of these soap stars, who would have time to "nuke" a TV dinner, clean the house, or run the kids around town?

# One Size Fits Most

Have you watched when a couple is in bed making out in the morning? The hair and makeup on both of them looks perfect. When have you slept in pencil-lined lips, mascara, and a dose of rouge on your face? And take notice—there isn't a hair on his head, or chest, out of place.

There are scenes when her collagen-injected lips meet his, as they kiss. It is enough to make you ask, "Where's the Scope?"

The same goes for reading a romantic novel. Imagine! The hero and heroine have traveled for weeks on the plains. They sleep and eat and struggle to survive, but neither one takes a bath! With no deodorant or toothpaste around, how did they deal with being around each other? Yet when we read that Thorn kissed Thelma and *"their sweet breath mingled, their beautiful hair glowed beneath the stars, his sparkling teeth gleamed in the moonlight, her soft legs* [with about a foot of fuzz on them?] *felt, oh so smooth, as her dainty feet peeped out from under her fifteen layers of crumpled petticoats."* All this after she woke up from her coma that had lasted eighteen chapters. Then he gently nibbled her tender lips (mind you they've been fried to a crisp in the hot blistering sun!). She hasn't eaten a thing for weeks. But she worries about how her hair looks? Don't forget the sweat and dirt he had sustained during all the hard work keeping her from danger. Still, his body reeks of cleanliness!

Suddenly, the goddess of romance is able to stand up all by herself. She is fit as a fiddle and ready to go on her journey with her lover without getting a checkup by her ex-lover, Doctor Feelgood, for possible malnutrition.

Will they live happily ever after, you wonder? She will bear him a dozen kids or so. Then she meets her lover's evil, handsome, long-lost twin from Whatchamacallit. They fall madly in love and she plots to discard brother number one. She dumps the hero who saved her comatose little hide from hell and back, and runs off with her newest schmuck. And so, another one bites the dust!

Whenever there isn't much going on on TV, I turn on a soap or I might even scan through a romantic novel and I realize how lucky I am. My hero comes home every night, even though the first thing he says is, "What's for dinner?" That's after he greets the dog!

He may not have a narrow waist, a great big hairy chest, or a ton of money. Perhaps he might reek if he didn't take a daily shower, but I wouldn't trade him for any soap character or romantic hero.

REAL LIFE SOAPS AND ROMANCE NOVELS WE DON'T NEED TO SEE.

HE WATCHED AS THE SWEAT FROM HER BROW ROLLED DOWN HER FACE AS SHE WASHED THE KITCHEN FLOOR. SURRENDERING TO AN URGE HE COULD NOT SUPPRESS ANY LONGER HE ASKED IN A BREATHLESS VOICE, "HONEY, WHAT'S FOR DINNER?"

**RULE #1 WHEN CONSIDERING A POOL: MAKE SURE YOURS IS NOT THE ONLY ONE IN THE NEIGHBORHOOD.**

# WHEN SCHOOL IS OUT

Look out, parents—the kids are home for summer vacation. All hell will break loose for the next few months. The schools will be closed and the kids will run your life.

Motorists are asked to slow down for the children's safety. In return we have to watch out for teens that might run us down while we're crossing the street.

Your college students will put a few gray hairs on your head by staying out all night, and when they finally show up at a ghastly hour you're not sure if you should throttle them or hug them with relief.

The money you'll be spending on food bills will triple, now that you're feeding the extra kids hanging around your house. How do you find time to clean, cook, and head out to your job? Many teenagers will be working this summer, while the younger crumb-crunchers have three months to drive Mom insane.

The kids also make plans with their buddies for sleepovers. That is, before they ask me, of course. But I'm a good egg and tell the friend he may stay a few nights. He gobbles up the evening meal cooked for Dad, and then tells me that his mom's food tastes a lot better than mine.

Unless I get a bus and hire a driver to cart the kids and their guests to their destinations, I will be the driver—leaving little time for myself. If you don't have a job outside of the home, people may think you are having too much fun vacationing with the kids. They will gladly send their kid to your house thinking you must be lounging around the swimming pool all day.

Public swimming pools have become a haven and a house of

# One Size Fits Most

God for many parents. The pools are a salvation for the duration of the summer vacation. The swimming pools stock up on life-guards, refreshments, and enough junk food to give kids' teeth a three-dimensional glaze. The kids' boom boxes blast head-banging tunes loud enough to make parents wish they'd followed the Halley's comet into space.

Of course, we pay a fortune for these summer activities.

Let's not forget the piles of dirty clothes. Not just your own kids', but for that other kid (what's his name?) who came over for a few nights and stayed the entire summer.

We can't leave the little kids home alone. Sure, it would be nice to take the kids to work. But the boss may not appreciate having little people drooling on the desks, or chewing on paper that has to make its way into the fax machine.

Babysitting is a good part-time business for teens. It gives them a sense of responsibility. Some businesses provide day-care centers at the workplace that will hire summer help.

What are the kids that do not have jobs, or are too young to work, going to do all summer long? They can attend summer camp for a few weeks, and visit relatives for short stays, even though some relatives might not welcome the little intruders.

We can't send them to boot camp.

Once upon a time Dad was the sole breadwinner bringing home the dough. Mom stayed at home kneading and baking the stuff and watching the kids. Sometimes Mom earned a few extra bucks by taking in a few kids to care for. She could use the money for a perm, or a new dress. But today's laws demand that when you take in a few kids it will cost you money. You must make your home kid-proof, have a license, and buy insurance for coverage worth a gazillion dollars.

It also takes plenty of parental guidance to keep kids safe and sound, and especially to keep them away from drugs. The slogan "Just say no" works on the little ones, but it is not enough to keep the bigger kids out of trouble.

The days of living close to grandparents has become a thing of the past for many families. Children are now spending more time with caregivers who are not family members.

Many young professional parents who have studied long, hard hours and have earned a degree find it very difficult to give up that job and the extra income in order to have one parent home with the kids. Our lifestyles and our needs have changed a great deal. Living expenses have made it virtually impossible for many to just be a stay-at-home parent.

Things may change someday. There has been talk about keeping schools open all year around. But for now, parents will have to keep their kids and their buddies busy during the summer break.

Suddenly, the summer will be over. The city will close its pools, and the kids will be back in school. We will have survived another summer vacation.

# HOUSE PETS

I have lived around pets all my life and am convinced I'd make a great zookeeper. My family seemed to always be outnumbered by things that crept, crawled, or slithered. Oftentimes it was "Animal Kingdom" at its best. At one point, my uncle brought home a cute little monkey from a faraway land. The poor thing never adjusted and died of pneumonia.

Over the years, we have sheltered cats, dogs, birds, baby mice, turtles, fish, and several cages filled with hamsters.

Sam, our adopted mutt, was the most talented of our pets. He could howl songs and knew how to dance for his Alpo®. Pete, the parrot, could imitate people's voices in several languages. Needless to say, we quickly learned never to discuss family gossip in front of him.

Marvin, Tilly, and Scooter, our three goldfish, were most unlucky when Biff, the cat, decided to go on his annual fishing expedition. The trio lost their lease on life. When we brought home new ones, Biff snatched them as well.

We inherited our dog Sam, and soon discovered he was deaf in both ears and had developed a chronic heart condition. He had come to us virtually toothless. Most of his teeth were so bad they had to be pulled the first day he arrived. Old Sam spent his remaining years on heart medicine and food prepared in a blender. He did, however, earn a reputation as "Stud," the neighborhood gigolo. Sam fathered a multitude of puppies. Apparently, teeth weren't a high priority for the neighborhood's female dogs.

Our cat, Biff, could never accept old Sam, and behaved in

spiteful ways. Biff spent his days making Sam's life miserable. He'd sneak up on the couch and, when Sam strolled by, Biff would pounce on top of him. Then, with his claws clamped tightly to Sam's furry coat, they'd race around the house until they both collapsed from exhaustion.

My kids loved to volunteer my time. A teacher at school needed someone to look after two pet turtles, George and Millie, during summer vacation. Naturally, our little animal sanctuary was eagerly offered. Our son then vowed he would take good care of them. Of course, you know the rest of the story on that.

During George and Millie's stay we met with a small crisis. One of the turtles seemed to have vanished from the aquarium. Frantically, I checked out Biff to see if he had anything to do with the disappearance. To my relief Biff hadn't had a turtle snack even though he looked guilty. I discovered later the turtle had been hiding beneath the sand in the aquarium. I slept easier when the two "shells" went back to school.

Sam passed away and we adopted Charlie. No one ever explained to Charlie that he was a dog. While he was small in stature, he was equipped with a gigantic bark and an awesome set of fangs. Charlie lived longer than all of our other pets put together.

After Charlie was gone I didn't want to own another pet. I had spent too much time loving and grieving for them. But the house has become a bit too quiet of late. Like many other people, I vowed to spare myself from feeling that loss again.

Recently, I met the cutest dog that looked so much like my old Charlie. As most animal lovers find, I missed the unconditional love a furry friend provides. It will be nice having a puppy chasing around the house again.

# HOLDING THE BAG

With spring just around the corner, I decided I could use a new handbag. I have been a handbag junkie forever, and have dozens of them stashed away. I always look over my shoulder to check out the latest brand names and styles. While I try to hold off, the thought of hunting for a new bag is so exhilarating I can't resist.

Usually, when I clean out my closet I have a tough time sorting through the bags. When I look at my "oldies" I just can't bring myself to get rid of them. Most have been part of my wardrobe at one time or another, and I couldn't dream of tossing out any of my favorites.

I also discovered I purchase too many black handbags because, after all, they go with anything. Even so, I still like to switch from one bag to another when the mood strikes.

I recently flipped through several fashion magazines and loved all the new spring colors and styles. However, spending $600 on a handbag is outrageous. Some cost more than a used car. They also weigh more than the models in the magazines.

The other day I started my big hunt for the bag of the season. I always search for bags that can hold my entire life inside of them. This includes storing my makeup for a week's survival, and my car phone. The bag must also be tough enough to hold toys, and an overload of cookies and crackers for the grandkids. But, of course, I still have to carry a stylish handbag. Some bags are so deep you can never find anything once you put it inside. You'll spend hours trying to locate your keys or your wallet. This is especially hard at the grocery store when you're in the checkout line trying to dig up your checkbook. The shoulder strap is also very important and can be a pain in the neck—literally. I don't like a strap made with a heavy metal chain that cuts off the circulation in your arm. It causes your fingers to tingle for hours. Then there is the one called "Le Sack" that is so heavy when filled, it makes you walk like a hunchback.

Other handbags look adorable, but barely hold your lipstick. Some designers are saying that the season's bag of the moment is soft, slouchy, and fit to be tied. My choices are tote bags with zippers, rather than a drawstring, just in case someone tries to lift your wallet.

I looked at a local department store and saw handbags in all sizes and shapes. I found a couple of nice ones, but I realized they didn't go with any of my outfits. They also didn't match my shoes. The only pair of shoes that matched came in a size 5.

I began another "bag" adventure and visited the boutique. There I found several handbags, and reasoned that I would find them a home. At another store I spotted some that looked so nostalgic—my mom used to carry those styles. I do like some of the old-fashioned bags. I have a few that are so old and worn I couldn't possibly give them away.

Some stores feature brand name look-alike handbags. They have the "look" but cost a lot less. These bags won't last as long as the real thing, but who wants to carry the same old bag forever?

Also, remember when you change your handbag be sure to transfer all the "stuff" you need to the new bag. I don't know how many times I've had to go home for my wallet and my credit cards.

This season I'm determined to go with a pastel handbag for a change. Maybe it is time for some of my retro bags to retire to a junkyard. Naturally, I'll have to shop for a few new pastel outfits to go with my new pastel handbag. Then, of course, I'll be obliged to find a pair of pastel shoes to match.

# I HAVE NOTHING TO WEAR

We've been invited to a wedding and I have absolutely nothing to wear! After having searched through my closets, I discover the outfits have already seen too many weddings in the last five years.

I make plans to go shopping for a new outfit. When I arrive at the store, I try on every dress and pantsuit in the place. The clerk waiting on me assures me that she will help me find that perfect look. That's easy for her to say—she couldn't possibly understand my problem. For the next hour I work my way in, and worm my way out, of the clothes. The zippers won't go up and the snaps keep popping. The clerk cheerfully explains that I may want to try something with a fuller cut to enhance my mature shape. (What she is really saying is I need a larger size.)

When she brings me an outfit with a psychedelic mushroom print, I wonder what designers are smoking when they create their fashions.

After a long time I give up and the clerk is relieved to see me exit the store.

The clothes I tried on made me feel out of touch, I certainly don't want to look like my daughter, but also don't want to spend more money on a dress than the cost of the wedding reception!

What are people wearing? I wonder. The lengths of the skirts are either too long or too short. Not every woman looks good in an ankle-length dress. Especially when she is short.

Length does count in the fashion world, both long and short. If you're planning to attend any future weddings or plan to buy a new wardrobe, check out the fashion designer's up and coming

# One Size Fits Most

styles for this fall. Designer Calvin Klein, whose collection featured plenty of evocative twists and turns, says longer lengths make for "a discreet element of drama."

Designer Oscar de la Renta is planning to bring back long skirts in a multi-colored patchwork version with fur trim at the hips! Unless you're tall and thin like singer Celine Dion, forget the furry hips.

So, will this new trend leave us with the long and the short of it? Has the fashion world forgotten about the women who don't look right in ankle-length dresses, or micro miniskirts? Do they realize that not all of us wear a size 6? Sometimes I'm convinced that fashion designers try to make us feel guilty for not wanting to wear the styles they dictate to us.

Let's hope that there are still fashion designers who understand that not everyone likes wearing long floor-sweepers that make a woman look downright dowdy. Maybe they can offer styles and lengths that will accommodate a normal woman's lifestyle.

When at last I find a suitable outfit, I still have to buy shoes and a matching handbag. I hate to put a lot of money into a pair of shoes and handbag for just one night. Especially after having seen those horrible shoes built on a platform. Try keeping your balance on a pair of platform shoes while dancing with your partner. Many stores offer to dye the shoes and handbag to match your outfit. But sometimes they'll turn out a different color that doesn't match your clothes.

Finding the right style can really be challenging. But there are several great shops in our area—including a petite shop. One can shop the world over and never find the things you want. You might be surprised to find that special outfit you've been looking for in your local dress shop.

Shopping should be a fun experience and doesn't always have to cost a fortune.

When I show up at the wedding in my new outfit, and people tell me how great I look, I might just tell them that I've had that outfit hanging in my closet forever!

# GARAGE SALES

Just the other day I was cruising the neighborhood, and I noticed the many garage sale signs along the side of the road. Curious to find out what kind of things people were buying and selling, I decided to stop and snoop around.

It was intriguing watching people bargaining over junk that seemed worthless to some and so valuable to others. People purchased things that looked better than the stuff I have accumulated over the years. I found several items that looked unique and bought them for practically nothing. Some people were bargaining over stuff that looked like trinkets Aunt Minnie left us in her will. With school starting soon, people were looking for kids clothes—especially blue jeans. Baby items such as furniture, toys, and clothes were also very popular. Our baby furniture was so outdated, the Salvation Army rejected the stuff!

When we held a garage sale a few early birds drove up—even before our doors were open. Piling out of their truck like commandos from a swat team they looked around quickly hoping to find valuable antiques. When they realized there were none, they made a quick exit. Did these people think I'd put out my Rembrandt and Vincent van Gogh paintings?

There are people who spend lots of time searching for old dishes, glassware, and table linens. Sometimes you might even find that special something you've been searching for. I guess that's the thought that keeps them going.

A friend of mine had been looking for anything in her dish pattern. She had purchased her set of dishes when she and her husband were stationed in Germany. On the trip back to the United

# One Size Fits Most

States, three of the place settings had been broken during shipping. Over the years she had called many shops around the country and she even wrote to the company that made them. These dishes meant a lot to her, but she had no luck in finding the extra pieces. The pattern had been discontinued. She loved going to garage sales and one day her luck changed. She nearly cried at what she saw. She had spotted her pattern. These were the exact same dishes she had been searching for. She never dreamed she would find her dishes again—let alone three place settings!

Exploring at garage sales is really a great pastime, especially when the whole neighborhood participates. Walking from one house to another is also good exercise. Lately, Beanie Babies have made their way to garage sales. People enjoy buying and trading their Beanie Baby collections. Garage sales also give people a chance to show off their talents. Like my friend who had talked me into going along with her. I really didn't want to go at first—what would I do with someone else's old junk? The stuff I had accumulated over the years I couldn't even give away. But my friend is one of the most talented people I know. She can sew a dress out of old kitchen towels, and whip up a skirt out of a couple of dinner napkins. She always looked at garage sales for old rundown furniture. She had found some old dilapidated chairs and she spent many hours stripping off the old coats of paint. It left the chairs so shaky it was as if they had a chill. Ultimately, she turned them into pieces of art. When she holds her annual garage sale many people are eager to buy her crafts.

One of my neighbors was a garage sale connoisseur. She would wait until the last day of the sale, and buy things at half off. On the following weekend she'd sell the stuff at her own garage sale for a small profit. Once a young boy caught up in the excitement offered to buy her dog.

Going to garage sales was fun. I have learned a lot about what junk I should hang on to—in case I ever decide to have another garage sale—and what junk is just junk. But the only way I will have another garage sale is when I am guaranteed to sell *all* of my old junk to buy all brand-new things. (And that probably won't happen in this lifetime.)

# CREEPY CRAWLERS & FURRY CREATURES

When we first moved to St. Charles, I wondered how I was going to adjust to living in a new town. It seemed like a friendly community and I was anxious to meet our neighbors and make new friends.

Soon we discovered we had friends everywhere—crawling out of the woods.

We had moved into a wooded area where insects the size of prairie dogs performed their nightly concerts. There were armies of spiders spinning webs in the nooks and crannies of our house. I ducked as bugs the size of helicopters buzzed over my head. The carpenter ants were so gigantic they could carry away the picnic table!

After negotiating with several local exterminators, we found one whose chemicals annihilated most of the unwanted intruders—if only for a short time. But the invaders always returned, bringing with them their swarms of creepy, crawling warriors.

One day while taking a break, I noticed a furry little creature scampering toward me. It was a squirrel staring at me with his large, round eyes. Hubby handed the creature a nut and within seconds the critter and the nut had disappeared. Minutes later the squirrel returned, bringing with him eight clones begging for more nuts.

In the months that followed, the squirrels would sit on the roof peeking through the windows. We sensed their presence as they waited for their breakfast. We tried to put some corn out, hoping they'd adjust to munching on less expensive snacks. In protest they started picketing our house demanding nuts. We had become so popular among our outdoor guests, even an occasional skunk would graze in our backyard and show his gratitude by leaving a trail of eau de parfum. Once in a while Bambi and his family passed through and lingered long enough to munch and rest.

Feeding these cute little "furry fluffers" had become quite costly. The squirrels felt so comfortable being our guests, they decided to take up residence in the attic. At first we thought the scratching and gnawing was mice. We borrowed Schmitty, a neighbor's cat. But he got scared and hid under the bed all day. We finally called the people from the wildlife control service and they confirmed that squirrels had, indeed, invaded our attic.

The squirrels had apparently chewed through the vents and worked their way into the attic. Since we didn't want to hurt the creatures, a cage was installed to catch them. The squirrels sensed that something was up. They waited behind the trees while watching us with humor as the cage remained empty. The end result was a lot of damage to our roof. Eventually, the squirrels forgave us for trying to oust them and they continued to show up for their meals.

A few weeks had passed, and one evening we heard something like chirping in the chimney. We thought the squirrels had discovered another entry to sneak back in. We called the chimney sweep, and they informed us that we had some new "friends." Many hours and a lot of money later, five baby raccoons were captured. They were put in a box and set on the roof where Mom was able to find her babies.

The following season, Mother Raccoon decided she was not about to give up her home. She chewed through the newly installed chimney cap and made her way back inside the chimney where she produced another batch of babies.

For a second time, the chimney sweep came to the rescue and retrieved the babies. A larger cap was placed over the chimney in hopes that this one would be stronger and keep our outdoor friends out. So far this year the chimney has no new tenants, and the new roof is holding up.

There are still many unidentified flying insects swooping

around. They've multiplied and grown larger each year, it seems. Some of these species look truly strange and can't possibly be from this earth.

We continue to feed the squirrels, and hang out with Bambi, and occasionally smell the aroma of Pepe Le Pew.

One can certainly tell spring has returned when new "friends" start visiting our home. They include our little buddies Chip and Dale, the chipmunks.

# One Size Fits Most

Come on, honey, now seriously,
what about this one?

*what about that?*
*I need that!*

You haven't worn this in years!

*But I might.*

How 'bout this? This has got to go.
It's falling apart!

*No way!*
*I've had that since*
*college!*

Yes, I know. That's why it's got to go!

PILE TO KEEP        PILE TO TOSS

# DEARLY-DEPARTED CLOTHES

Have you ever wondered why some people spend so much time cleaning out their closets? With fall approaching, cleaning my closets is one of my big projects. Cleaning closets is a way of letting go of the old and bringing in the new.

My problem is letting go of my old clothes, even though they no longer fit like they once did. When I clean my closets, I just transfer all my out-of-season clothes to another closet. I always have hopes that I might fit into them, or that they may come back in style.

Every season I vow that I will make more space in my closets. My intention is to bag up the old clothes and give them away to some good cause. But I always find myself slipping back into my old habit.

When the kids moved out, there was lots of empty space in the closets. I had promised hubby that he could have an extra spot for his clothes. Unfortunately, that promise has been broken as the empty spaces were filled up with things I'd probably never use again.

Having a garage sale was one solution. Some neighbors and friends got together, bringing an abundance of stuff for the big sale.

Soon we were admiring each other's treasures. My closets and drawers filled up in less time than it took to pour a cup of coffee that day. I was in the same predicament as before the garage sale.

I scoured through a heap of clothes I intended to give away. There were several outfits that had fit a much slimmer frame once upon a time, sweaters that were so old they had fur balls

# One Size Fits Most

all over them, and shoes that were smaller in size than my feet. Clearly, I realized, that time and gravity offered me little sympathy. It was time to part with them.

It occurred to me that I had spent so much time cleaning out closets, and accomplished so little. I called a friend who worked in a local clothing store. She took one look at my clothes, and convinced me that only a swarm of desperate hungry moths would be caught with these things. It was time to let go of my "golden oldies."

With her help and wisdom she showed me how to make the best use of my closets. We went shopping and purchased several large plastic boxes with lids. We wrapped most of the sweaters in tissue paper, which helps keep them from being crushed, and added a touch of scented sachet to keep the sweaters from smelling stale. We put them in the plastic boxes and stored the boxes under the bed, allowing me more room in the closets. We used hangers that held several pairs of slacks, or skirts, and a shoe tree that held up to 12 pair of shoes. (Shoe trees can also hold scarves and other accessories.) And she reminded me, "When you don't wear your clothes for more than a year, get rid of them!"

When we had finished cleaning and bagging up my old clothes, I noticed that I really did have more room. There was only one thing left to do. It just so happened the store my friend worked at was having one of the biggest sales of the season. Could I honestly refuse to pick up some of those bargains? I did have all that extra space in my closet.

I have finished my closet cleaning for this season. My old stuff has found a new home, and my new bargains look great in my clean closet. I only hope the next time I do my closet cleaning, I will be able to part with my "new" old clothes.

# MAIL FOR SALE

Receiving mail from friends and family has always been an important part of our lives. Some people hate to write letters and prefer to talk on the phone, or chat on the Internet. But most of us go to the mailbox to retrieve our daily batch of mail. We rummage through stacks of papers to find a letter from our loved ones. Especially around the holidays and birthdays.

When we returned from a recent trip, I dropped by the post office to pick up the mail. The amount was so huge I could have lined the kitty litter box for an entire year. After sorting through the piles of advertisements and free coupons we filled up several garbage bags with unwanted junk mail. I hated to give up a free weekend trip to the health spa, and a coupon for an experimental hair transplant treatment. Unfortunately, I didn't dare throw out any bills. They go into the hideaway pile until they get paid.

So much advertising is done through the mail. Companies send out tons of catalogs so people can order the items they want. I usually look forward to getting my favorite catalogs and magazines. They help to provide information on what is new in medicine and in fashion. I even like the free trial-size soaps and stuff for my home. I just don't enjoy carrying the extra pounds of junk mail.

When the volume of mail doesn't fit inside the mailbox, our very kind mailman will ring the doorbell and hand us our mail, even in bad weather. Each day there seems to be more mail, and the mailbox seems to have shrunk because there is not enough room for all the mail anymore. My mailbox droops from the overload. When does mail become junk mail? Sometimes I think we are on some kind of hit list from every company in the world.

# One Size Fits Most

According to the postmaster, the post office in our town receives approximately 400,000 pieces of mail per week. That comes to about eleven pieces of mail per household each day, including businesses in the area.

During the summer months, I'm told, the flow of mail slows down. The volume of mail increases from September through December. Mother's Day and Christmas are two of the biggest mail days.

A lot of people like shopping by mail from catalogs. This saves time for those who don't have the time to go shopping in the stores. Some people like to clip out the coupons and recipes from fliers and magazines. The bargain hunters want to be kept informed when sales occur. The newspapers are a great source for coupons when it comes to events, sales, and places to dine. So why do some people get annoyed when their mailboxes are over-stuffed with mail? People like to sign up for a contest or a drawing, they give out their name and address. I stay away from signing up for things and avoid giving out my address. But that doesn't seem to solve the problem; the junk mail still finds our mailbox.

How many times have you received a document that looked official? When you opened the letter it stated that you are eligible to win a free ten-day trip. It tells you just fill out your name and you will be flown to some remote place. When you reply you end up getting more mail, and companies happily sell your name and address to other companies.

Getting a lot of junk mail and sorting through heaps of unwanted advertising can be a nuisance for the elderly, because some folks don't know which pieces of mail are important to keep and which ones are not.

There will always be people who enjoy digging through the piles of junk mail just to find that special bargain. They'll enjoy reading about upcoming events and freebies they receive in their mailbox. I do hope that someday my name will be chosen for a lottery and that they will contact me by mail. I promise when that happens I won't complain about having to sort through the piles of junk mail.

# RAGING THROUGH THE HOLIDAYS

I've been standing in the checkout line at the grocery store for what seems like an hour. That was after having shoved my way through the crowded aisles. With Thanksgiving coming up, everyone is rushing to finish their grocery shopping. People are in such a hurry they're slamming their grocery carts into each other. It's almost like being in a demolition derby!

Standing in the long line watching my ice cream melt, I notice some crabby person in front of me getting impatient and looking like she's about to have a fit of shopping rage.

A young mother with her three children is trying to hold on to her sanity while keeping her tykes from destroying the candy shelves. The fifteen people behind me are looking as if they're going to go "postal."

Someone starts complaining loudly about the snail-like pace. Another angry voice shouts, "Can't you people move it? I'm in a hurry." (Isn't everyone, I wonder?) One inconsiderate person thinks by creeping up closer behind me the line will move faster. I am packed in so tight, standing in line for so long, the aroma of stale eau de parfum is starting to cause my eyes to itch.

My heart goes out to the poor checkout person who has to deal with this angry mob. The poor kid bagging my groceries is becoming so nervous he drops a huge turkey on the floor, breaking the bird's legs and enraging its new owner. So furious is the recipient of the injured fowl she demands to speak to the manager. The bagger offers to clean the bird off after its fall on the floor.

Sneaking over to another checkout counter is tempting—but

# One Size Fits Most

the sign says, "15 items or less and cash only." Since I have more than 15 items and no cash I'm out of luck. People behind me would count my 17 items and give me an angry look.

The customer in the express checkout line fumbles desperately for her checkbook and her preferred customer card. As she nervously digs in her oversized purse the people behind her are not amused. They grow more frustrated and tempers are flaring. People's patience is on edge and you can sense trouble brewing in the air.

Finally, it is my turn, I can't wait to check out and make my escape.

At last I'm headed toward my car. With all the hassle I went through I didn't realize my car is almost out of gas.

At the gas station, people are busy occupying every gas pump. The lines are long and move more slowly than ketchup out of a bottle. People look discontented having to wait their turn. I wonder, what's the rush? Lots of folks are about to sit in their car for a few hours making their way to Grandma's house. This time having to wait at the pump may be cherished once on the road. One can hear people grumbling and cursing while waiting to fill their tanks with gas. This is supposed to be the spirit of Thanksgiving?

I wonder why people are so uptight during the holidays. Have you ever waited for the elevator doors to open while at the mall? People will push the button over and over, thinking this will make the elevator come faster. Most people are usually very polite and courteous at their place of work, or at holiday parties. But when these same people have to stand in line and wait, they become irritable and cranky.

It seems everyone is forgetting the meaning of sharing and the importance of giving. Let's not rush through this special time— let's enjoy the spirit of Thanksgiving!

# A "FOWL" THANKSGIVING

Thanksgiving always brings back memories of when I created my first turkey dinner. It was a masterpiece! A crispy, one-of-a-kind, burnt-to-a-cinder bird!

I've since spent years torching, scorching, and mutilating turkeys—but I have finally earned some credibility for baking the bird to perfection.

I've used many gadgets and tricks to cook the turkey. I had cooking sessions with Betty Crocker, Campbell's Soup, Duncan Hines, cookbooks, and several trips to the local grocery store. I finally learned how to do it right. But, like many young brides, my first experience turned out to be a total disaster.

I remember receiving a gift certificate from my hubby's company as a gift. With my free turkey card, I picked out the biggest one from the freezer at the grocery store—the thing was huge!!

Now, I have never been good at following directions, but I read the instructions several times and felt I was ready to go to work. (A first grader could stuff this thing, I thought.) Not sure which side of the turkey was up, my husband demonstrated for me by lying flat on his back and holding out his arms and legs.

I put the bird on the kitchen counter, and prepared myself for some leisurely cooking. It seemed so easy. The directions simply read, "Fill up the larger cavity of the turkey with the ready-made stuffing." (*Do turkeys have bad teeth, I wondered?*) And what is stuffing supposed to look like anyway? I double-checked the little pamphlet that had been inserted inside the hind-end of the creature. It stated that you can chop up the gizzard, neck, and liver and use them in the stuffing. I looked, but couldn't find the

# One Size Fits Most

neck and giblets.

I wasn't about to call my mom for advice. She was convinced that I could never raise kids or look after a husband, let alone cook a meal! She thought I'd probably shorten the lives of my family by poisoning them. Well, I thought, I'd show her!

I dug up some stale old bread that had enough greenish tinge on the edges to make the bread look festive. (I found out later this pretty green stuff is also called mold.) I mixed some spices together and added it to the bread crumbs. When that was done, I had no idea if it was right—it looked like ground-up mush.

Next I tried to clean the turkey, but it was still frozen. How was I to know it took days to thaw this bird? When I realized there was no way I could get the ground-up mush inside the frozen bird, I dumped the goop into a separate dish and put it alongside the turkey. Believe me when I tell you it took two days to cook that !@#$% bird! The oven was set at 350° but I still sat up most of the night waiting for this huge beast to cook.

After two days of pacing, I decided the turkey must have cooked long enough. I took the pan with the torched bird out of the oven—poor soul—it was a pitiful sight! I knew I could never show this disaster to my hubby. The turkey was all black and shriveled in the pan. It was way past Cajun. The drumsticks looked like sawed-off stumps, and its wings so were badly shattered. I felt sorry for the turkey—it didn't deserve to be burnt to a mass of hot lava rock.

I buried it in the backyard and said a nice prayer in hopes that it would have a more pleasant afterlife. The best dishes I fixed that day were the mashed potatoes, the rolls, canned cranberry sauce, and the Betty Crocker cheesecake.

But I still don't know where I went wrong with the dressing. It looked as if the pan had permanent rust spots on it.

Some husbands are very understanding—and some are not—when you've turned this special holiday into a horrible nightmare. Mine got me through Thanksgiving that first year.

And still every now and then I mess up—like overcooking the dressing, or burning the buns, or even botching up the potatoes. But, I haven't buried any more turkeys in the backyard!

# ENVY WHO?

My next door neighbor just bought a brand-new sports car and it's sitting in his driveway making me green with envy. He also takes his family on a cruise twice a year. It seems as if these people have money to burn.

One of my co-workers lives in a lovely big house with a swimming pool and has a sailboat twice the size of my house. I always wondered what he really does for a living. Nevertheless, I'm envious and ask myself why some people have everything and we don't. Do you find yourself wanting the lifestyle these people have?

Some people, it seems, have all the luck while we're struggling to make ends meet. I know people who have money and those who pretend they have it. Take a closer look at the people who pretend they're wealthy. It may not be all it is cracked up to be.

There is an old saying, "Be careful what you wish for—you might get it." You probably think the neighbor driving the expensive sports car is rich, or the co-worker in that huge house must be fortunate to live in such a place.

There once was a family who had everything money could buy. They had several homes and five brand-new cars, one for each member of the family. Everyone envied them. Dad appeared to have a fantastic job and was a board member of the local country club. Mom stayed home raising the children with the help of a nanny. She was also deeply involved organizing fundraisers, and served on several important committees in the community. She was dressed to kill and dripping in jewelry that would have made Elizabeth Taylor envious.

# One Size Fits Most

Their two children were well-mannered and attended private schools. They even each got their own car on their 16th birthday. Everything seemed like smooth sailing for this seemingly wealthy family. This brought out the green-eyed monster in some folks who believed they were less fortunate.

Did they think just because it appeared these people had money to spend that they were really rich? Perhaps these people just might want others to think they were wealthy. Sometimes it is hard to suppress our desire to have a new sports car like the neighbor's car. Or, we want to live in a larger home. We all want bigger and better things. When a friend buys a big house we would like to go out and buy a bigger house, too. But how are we going to pay for it?

I wonder how some people can afford to spend so much on cars and homes. Obviously, there are people who live all their lives on borrowed money. They charge everything on their credit cards and worry about making payments later. After a time things start to catch up with them and the chickens come home to roost.

Take the guy who has been driving the sports car I've been envious of. He owed so much money to his creditors he had to file for bankruptcy. The co-worker with the beautiful house and swimming pool had to put the house up for sale. I guess he couldn't make the payment when he lost his job due to a drinking problem.

Unfortunately, the family with the fabulous estate homes and fantastic jewelry lost everything gambling on the cruises. Mom was forced to go to work and the kids had to take jobs after school to make their car payments.

The moral of this story is "don't give in to the green-eyed monster." Don't wish for the things you don't have. Earn them one at a time. You may think money will give you status. But nothing that is worth anything in this life comes gratis.

# FACE-LIFT CREAMS

Whenever I go shopping at a mall I try to avoid some of the departments.

For example, you happen to walk past a makeup and perfume counter and some clerk sticks a jar of cream under your nose, or spritzes your body with some new cologne. Naturally, the person shoving the lotions and creams in your face is younger than your own daughter. Yet, these kids act like experts on how to slowdown your aging process. They tell you how you ought to smell good to make your loved one happy.

If that were true, I'd have a makeup and perfume spa built in my home. Right! My loved one is so allergic to fragrances, that if I came home with the stuff sprayed all over my body, he'd go into an aroma-coma. He'd breakout in golf ball-sized hives! If the makeup and creams they are trying to sell us are going to keep us looking as young as they say it will, their own mothers must look like their younger sisters!

I try to not hurt the clerks' feelings and I do like to get some of the free samples offered, so I let the person talk me into slopping pounds of firming lotion and wrinkle reduction creams on my face and thighs, even though I explain to her that last week I spent hundreds of dollars on a previously recommended skin care product with the same brand name.

The young person looks at me in amazement and tries to explain to me that these newest products are manufactured in Shcromboliriskia, a country I've never heard of, and that this skin cream, which happens to be made from sheep extractions, is the best facial cream every produced!

# One Size Fits Most

The clerk reads the ingredients stated on the back of these creams with words I can't pronounce. *"Now, these radical scavengers will exfoliate the dead cells that muddy your complexion, to promote pore breathe-ability."* By the time she has applied new under cream, in-between cream, night cream, after-night cream, and morning cream, a ton of liner for lids and brows, and a touch of color on my belly button, I won't be able to afford the dress I came to the mall to buy for my child's graduation.

Every time I go back into some of the same stores, another person tells me she can help me take years off my face if I use her new products today. What about the creams I purchased last week? I was told those creams were to last at least a year. (Dream on!) They're going to show me how to look thirty again. (Yeah, right!) I would love to have a face that looks like a thirty-year-old. What will they do with the rest of my body to match my thirty-year-old face? (I wonder.)

The sales people will swear by these new products, and want to sell you years' worth of them. Every time you go back to the store they will vouch that this latest wonder cream will keep its promise and that this time the years of aging will disappear forever.

We still want to believe in miracles and hope that maybe this newest product will give us a more youthful look. My drawers contain enough anti-wrinkle creams and anti-aging products to fill up Soldier's Field.

We will always keep looking for that fountain of youth that is sold in bottles and jars. Many of us will always believe that somewhere out there are products that will give us eternal youth, and a firmer body with little, or no, exercise. For now, we'll buy tons of beauty products and vitamins to help us feel and look better. By the time we finally retire—and can no longer hop, skip, and jump—we will still have the memories of how much time we wasted worrying about our looks.

# EQUALITY?

BUT, I STILL WANT TO BE
TREATED LIKE A PRINCESS!

When you pick up a magazine and read the articles about how to get along with the opposite sex, you've got to wonder who writes these things! Advice columns, television programs, and radio talk shows are always preaching about how men and women should treat each other.

We're told that men should treat women with respect and dignity. Women are demanding equal opportunities in their careers, and competing with men for better paying jobs. Can't a woman accomplish anything a man can?

Women are joining the armed forces and are willing to fight on the front lines. They have been attending colleges and clubs that previously only accepted men. For many years women have been performing much of the work that most men thought only they were capable of doing. Women are pumping iron at health clubs, pumping gas in their cars, they can change a tire, and they can (*and do*) bring home the bacon. Women have shown they can hold their own.

But do all women want to be *treated* the same as men? Being treated the same doesn't necessarily mean *acting or looking* the same. Let's compare a few things. Imagine a woman dressed up in a gorgeous gown walking around sporting a beer belly. A man can carry his potbelly wherever he goes. Would anyone make a fuss and offer him a girdle with a built-in tummy control?

When a woman finds one gray hair on her head, friends are quick to lend their advice on what color she ought to use to cover up her little secret. Her hairstylist will urge her to lighten her hair a few shades to diminish crow's-feet around the eyes. But when

# One Size Fits Most

his hair turns gray around the temples, doesn't he look great? Those creases on his face give him character. On her face they're considered extra mileage.

When a man's hair starts to recede he's told bald is beautiful. When a woman loses her hair, she panics.

At some point in time the eye doctor recommends glasses for him, everyone says he looks distinguished. But when she gets fitted for glasses, she fears this is the beginning of middle age and menopause.

We see an older man dating a younger woman, people marvel how lucky she is to have found such a distinguished, mature man. But, if she even *thinks* of going out with a younger man she is having a midlife crisis.

If a man comes into work looking grim-faced, it is assumed he is having a bad day. Let a woman walk through the door without a smile and she'll stand accused of having PMS.

Can there ever be equality between men and women? Will we see women playing for professional football teams wearing armored breastplates for protection? Do we want to? One thing is for sure, there are differences between men and women.

Personally, I don't have a problem being treated differently than a man. I also believe that not all women and men expect to be treated equal. Many women still enjoy having a man open the door, pay for dinner, pump the gas, and drive her home.

I really dig it when my man shovels the snow, takes out the garbage, and changes a tire on the car. I also like it when he chops the wood and builds a cozy fire. He can still impress me by mowing the lawn, lifting heavy objects, and protect the family home from being invaded. I sure don't mind when he climbs a ladder to paint the outside of the house and replaces the gutters.

I also don't think most women would have a problem when her man helps put the kids to bed and washes the dishes. Equality is not about women playing football, changing a tire, or plucking out the gray hairs. There is a mutual respect to accepting our differences.

And, unless a man can become pregnant and give birth to a child, or a woman looks attractive growing beard, some of us don't feel the need to be equal with a man.

# WHERE'S MY STASH?

A few weeks ago I came home with a few bargains I had purchased. I had promised hubby to go easy on the spending, so I decided to hide my treasures someplace until the smoke cleared. Days later when I looked for my treasures, I couldn't remember where I had stashed the stuff. I nearly trashed the house trying to find them. I looked in every closet nook and cranny and even under the beds. But I couldn't find my stash. I became so involved tearing the place apart I had almost forgotten what I was looking for.

Occasionally we all misplace something, then when we forget about it, it usually turns up somewhere. After my friend's dad passed away, I helped clean up the house before they put it on the market. Members of the family spent days trying to track down his personal belongings, things like his checkbook and other important papers. We searched everywhere and when we finally located his things we were surprised. My friend's dad had a habit of hiding things in his dresser drawers. Among the stuff we found were several legal documents, important papers, and several bundles of socks stuffed with cash he had saved. Obviously, he didn't believe in putting his money in the bank and maybe he eventually forgot where he had hidden it.

Sometimes I buy things like that nifty little outfit I just had to have. I put it someplace safe and when I look for it I can't remember where I put it. Only to find it much later when it no longer fits, or is in style.

Sometimes people hide stuff they purchase strictly out of fear. One of my friends had been warned by her husband to stop

# One Size Fits Most

spending so much money. Their credit cards were charged to the max. With tears in her eyes she vowed to her beloved that she would be very careful about her spending habits. A few days later she was asked to go shopping with one of her friends. What harm would there be in picking up a few bargains, she thought.

While shopping they came upon an irresistible sale. When she paid for her things she put part of the sale on several credit cards and wrote a check for the remaining amount. That way both credit cards didn't look so bad when hubby got them. That afternoon when she returned home hubby was there. She was fearful and thought she'd better conceal her stash fast before entering the house. She decided to hide her goodies in a large plastic garbage bag and just leave it in the garage.

Unbeknownst to her, hubby wanted to be nice and took out the garbage that night. The following morning my friend was panic-stricken because she realized her new clothes had been taken outside with the other garbage bags. She also forgot which garbage bag contained her clothes.

How could she run outside and check each and every bag of garbage while her husband worked at home that day? She devised a plan and called her next door neighbor, asking her to rummage through the garbage bags. There were about nine bags sitting by the curb. Thankfully, the neighbor retrieved the right bag before the garbage truck pulled up.

I hope I remember what it was I bought and where I stashed it. I just can't remember what I had to hide. When I find it I just hope that whatever the thing was it will still be something I really wanted!

# WORN-OUT OLD PANTS

Several weeks ago, our neighbors were preparing for a garage sale. It made me think about having one myself. I realized that in the last ten years we had accumulated a lot of things that we didn't need. Especially some of my hubby's old clothes.

A lot of women would love to go through their spouse's closets, discard their raggedy-looking clothes, and put them in a garage sale. Men will hang on to their old grubbies as long as their wives will let them.

Remember the times when he told you he didn't like your outfit? You ran out all upset and changed your clothes just to please him. But what about the stuff he wears? Especially clothes so outdated even the Salvation Army has rejected them.

Did you ever say to your husband, "I hope you never wear those pants and that ugly shirt again." He will probably say to you that he happens to like his ugly old clothes and feels very comfortable wearing them.

Wanting to help him out, you'll offer that you're going shopping with him to buy some new clothes. Imagine the look on his face! He'd rather submit himself to a root canal at the dentist's office than go shopping for clothes. He'd prefer a new TV or a fishing pole to go with his favorite old pants. There are times when he asks you to help him coordinate his shirts to go with the colors of his pants.

Now, I've seen men who dress very fashionably. But I've also seen a man at a friend's gathering wearing socks to match a necktie decorated with abstract art. The colors were so scary, it frightened their pregnant cat into premature labor.

# One Size Fits Most

It is true there are guys that just don't like to take the time to go shopping for clothes. Some loathe having to try on clothes in a store and having to wait in line to pay for their purchases. They'd prefer that their wife pick out their wardrobe. Besides, some men probably don't know the difference between their neck size and the length of their sleeves when they buy a shirt.

And unless you throw out his old clothes and furnish him with new ones, he will stick with the old through thick and thin. Letting go of his ancient attire would be like losing an old friend. He'll scream bloody murder, particularly if you dare toss out his favorite over-stretched ill-fitting pants, or the shirt he's worn since your first date. He says that his size hasn't changed, even though he has gained at least four pant sizes and blames you for shrinking his shirts. He'll never admit that his waistline is now below his belly button.

Shortly before we moved to Illinois we held a garage/garbage sale. I emptied hubby's closets and drawers to get rid of clothes that had been manufactured before President Theodore Roosevelt took office. I also gathered some of his old shoes that were so dilapidated our dog was afraid he'd hurt his teeth chewing on them.

I had promised my hubby we'd shop for new shoes and some new clothes that would make him look and feel great. That did not change the fact that he still didn't like to go shopping. There must be a way to get your spouse to go into a store.

When a man does go shopping it is usually an emergency—like a suit for a funeral or casual wear for a holiday. Of course, he'll wait until the last minute and when he feels guilty enough he rushes out to buy something from the wrong place in the wrong size and he ends up spending too much money.

I guess we should consider ourselves lucky that we don't have to depend on the guys to do the shopping!

# LET'S TIE ONE ON

Have you ever purchased a tie? Now, buying a tie is no big deal, if you know what you're looking for. But finding just the right tie can be a real bummer.

First of all, have you seen the latest craze in ties? Some look like pictures from the wild animal kingdom. Others have checks, polka dots, and paisley prints with boxer shorts to match! There are ties that look spray painted with street graffiti.

Basically, most men like to dress up without a tie. But since etiquette and management commands professionals wear a tie at the workplace, they must comply with their dress code.

A tie does, however, have several good uses. When eating in a restaurant, one can mop the food off his mouth with his tie, or catch the drinks he spills. He can use it to suppress a coughing or sneezing fit before splattering it all over his companion. He can wipe the grease from his hands, or fiddle with it when he's nervous.

The down side of owning a tie is having to clean it. Have you ever tried to wash and press the thing? I have taken them to the dry cleaner but with the money I spent on a couple of cleanings, I could buy a new one. Also, oftentimes they can't get the grease spots out and charge me for it anyway.

Sometimes a tie can cause major problems. The thing gets caught in an elevator door, or sucked into a garbage disposal. Do avoid mixing drinks in an electric blender while wearing a tie. Especially when mixing a mai-tai.

Many people have problems finding the right tie. The manufacturers keep changing the style every season. You'll see ties

# One Size Fits Most

with patterns of Pinocchio and Gepetto, Dopey, Sneezy, and Grumpy. But hubby only wears the ones with stripes, and these are hard to come by. They are virtually not available on this planet. I'll try a garage sale and maybe I can get some good old striped ties.

Years ago, I decided to make a tie for hubby. I was proud of my accomplishment. When I presented him with my gift he tried not to laugh and complimented me on my achievement. Years later, he still chuckles whenever he remembers my handiwork.

I did have some luck finding old ties on a discontinued tie rack in the back room of a men's store. I purchased every striped tie on the rack.

Cleaning up the house one day, I realized there are many uses for old retired ties. I found some that were so outdated, even hubby refused to wear them, so I made kites for the kids. The ties that were red, white, and blue made a great-looking flag.

I remember in the '70s when the men had little or no use for ties. They wore leisure suits, bell-bottoms, and those creepy looking love beads. It sure gave the old tie a long overdue rest.

The tie has changed, but the old striped banner is still worn by those men who won't go with the flow.

Of course, there are guys who want to look "stylish". They will wear some of the goofiest-looking ties. What about the good old bow tie? Two well-known men wore those bow ties. Former Senator Paul Simon and Orville Redenbacher, the master of popcorn. By the way, Orville's bow tie had stripes on it. Does Paul Simon's have stars? I wonder if the two men were related? There was a close resemblance.

Will the tie ever go out of style? I doubt it. Some fashion designers might give the tie another break. Most likely someone will come up with a new line of ties to knot.

So, if a man "ties one on," so to speak, even though you don't like the new look, hang on to the old ones—they may come back in style again.

# HAIR TODAY IS TOMORROW'S FUTURE

Where do we find the best salon to get our hair styled? And how do we know what is the right look for us? With today's busy lifestyles, simple haircuts are important for both women and men. We want to spend as little time as possible on our hair and wardrobe. At the same time, we want to look our very best.

When I worked in a hair salon, the only clientele we served were women and children. And when hair color was applied to the customer's hair, we worked mostly behind closed doors to hide our client's messy little secret.

As for men in the 1960s, having their hair cut, permed, or dyed in a beauty salon was rare. They'd either go to a barbershop or have their spouse cut their hair—which usually looked as if a bowl was placed on their heads. I could always tell when a friend cut hubby's hair—it looked as if it was sheared off by dull garden clippers. He'd wear a turtleneck for weeks to hide the back of his neck.

Nowadays men can find their fountain of youth and beauty as well as the women. A man doesn't have to sneak shoe polish on his temples anymore, or dip his head into his wife's leftover hair dye.

Men today look very polished without putting on the polish. Many professional businessmen go for facials, massages, and manicures. Health clubs are overflowing with guys signing up to work out at least three times a week. Today's man doesn't mind spending money to look his best.

A lot of men are short on time, but not all are short on hair. Some guys still want to look like the long, golden-tressed Fabio, who appears on the cover of romance novels. I'm sure these guys spend a ton of cash getting their hair frizzled and frazzled.

Fads come and go, but cleanliness still ranks high for most of us. Many professional people prefer smart and clean-looking hair. But sometimes we try to model ourselves after famous people—even if that look is not in our best interest. There are people who carry pictures of the latest stars—wanting to look like them. At the salon where I worked a woman once said, "I want my hair styled just like Cindy Crawford." Upon hearing this, my boss hollered, "Get the hot plate started! I'll get the wax!" This was meant in fun and the woman responded with equal humor, promising to lose 30 pounds.

Sometimes a miracle is needed when someone messed up their hair with a home perm or hair-coloring kit. Frantically the person will run to a hair salon and hope the hairstylist can fix the damaged hair. On those occasions the stylist has to perform an act of magic. They become the surgeon who has to repair the badly treated hair. The stylist can usually successfully shear off the frizzy ends, condition the hair back to health, and the client will be happy—and most will likely become a steady customer. It is worth the extra money going to a professional hair salon. When people have had a bad experience with a haircut, and they are afraid to go to just any hair salon, the advice is: Do some research when looking for a new hair salon. You might want to try a light trim first with a new stylist, before you have chemicals applied to your skin and hair. It is all right to look for specials. Some hair salons advertise a discount on haircuts or hair care products. This is great—just don't try to get the cheapest haircut. A good haircut is essential for both men and women. When you receive a good haircut, your hair should be easy to manage.

It is also important to feel secure with your stylist before you decide to perm or color your hair. Ask around and find out who gives the best haircuts. Word of mouth seems to be the best advertising. Before having your hair cut and styled, always check out the stylist's own hairdo and appearance. Why would you take advice on how to wear your hair when theirs looks like the return of Frankenstein's bride?

Also, pay attention on how much quality time the stylist spends on your hair. If the stylist rushes you through like pennies rolling through a coin machine, don't go back. That person didn't care about your hair.

The most important thing about having your hair cut and styled is that you're satisfied. You should feel like a million bucks rather than those pennies that run through the coin machine.

TWO FOR THEM, ONE FOR ME...

# SPIRIT OF GIVING... OR SCROOGE?

Every year I find myself facing the same dilemma—what to buy everyone for Christmas and how much I can spend on each person.

And, of course, I vow each year that only so much money will be spent on each family member. In order to save money, most friends are out. The nieces, nephews, and in-laws are outlawed. But I still have to buy for Grams and Gramps, the babysitter, the paperboy, the mailman, my best friends, and don't forget kitty and Fido!

The family has grown over the last few years, and it will continue to multiply and mutate. So has the gift list. Yet, I have to ask myself—what does Christmas really mean? How much do I want to spend on each member of the family? Christmas is for giving, so what does one give to the elderly relatives? Grandpa Otis and Grandma Bessie already own every trinket on this planet.

What about my newly-married children? They already received lots of household goods when they got married. Money is their greatest need. It has been said that giving money is not within the Christmas spirit. (Are they kidding?) When I got my gifts for Christmas last year I was delighted. Hubby gave me three gift-wrapped packages, each containing something green—money! I was overjoyed. Now I could go to the stores and hit all the after-Christmas sales, and buy the goodies I wanted to get myself.

In the meantime I still have to decide how much I am going to spend on my loved ones. I know I must stick to my budget and buy things that are useful and not too expensive.

There was a time when I could pick up a free gift with my

# One Size Fits Most

purchase from a grocery store. I would buy a bottle of detergent with a little puppet attached. They also gave away toys, hair products, and other useful gifts. I used them for stocking stuffers. Nowadays, everything has a big price tag. The freebies are no longer free. Today one has to buy lots of groceries in order to get a so-called free trinket, which you still have to pay for.

Some department stores give away a free turkey when you buy $100 worth of clothes. Poultry is pretty inexpensive, so, why would I spend $100 to get an $8 bird? And probably some off-beat brand name I've never heard of before.

The department stores also have their free tote bags filled with trial-sized items, such as cologne and makeup. I have to spend at least $50 in order to receive these gifts. Unfortunately, I can't give these trial-sized mini cheapies as presents to anybody; people will know I got them free.

In previous years I have sworn that this year we're cutting back on gifts, but when the holidays roll around and I go out and see all the Christmas lights and stores filled with beautiful things, my resolution, which I vowed I'd keep, tends to slip away. I feel such joy in buying things for my family, yes even my friends, because it's the season to be generous. Even though my deflated checkbook and over-extended credit cards may haunt me after the holidays, and drag my giving spirit back to reality.

I know that next year I will say the same thing about cutting back on gifts. I know that I will keep that promise as well as when I promised to keep my weight off—and that's a promise I have yet to keep!

# A NEW YEAR'S SOLUTION TO A RESOLUTION

I've made my latest New Year's resolution (again).

Like so many times before, I vow that this time I'll stick to it like peanut butter on a piece of bread. Uh huh! Except the bread would get soggy and my resolutions would drip right through the slice. So I look for loopholes and ways around the problems I have to face up to.

How do I keep my promises? Some of the most popular resolutions include trying the latest diet and exercise programs, and giving up that nasty cigarette habit that everyone, including the dog, hates.

Watching the tube and buying self-help books never seem to work well for me. Going to a doctor would be the better way to start out. But most importantly, it is up to me. I'm the person that can help myself the most. There are several good possibilities out there that can help me get started. Such as having the willpower and taking one day at a time.

Willpower is probably one of the most elusive qualities. I have the potential, but it stays tucked away. I keep thinking I don't have the strength to succeed. That will be the biggest part of my success in whatever problems I have to face in the next few months, and the rest of my life. Willpower is my strongest ally to help me achieve almost anything I set my mind to.

When I first decided to give up my cigarette habit, it scared the stuffing out of me. The thought of never being able to indulge in a cigarette again made me break out in hives. Especially those first few days. My thoughts were: *"What if I can't keep the promise I made to my children and my friends? What will they think of me?*

# One Size Fits Most

That was the first mistake I made. Never promise anyone that you're going on a diet, or that you're attempting to give up a bad habit, because people will hold you to that statement, and that puts extra pressure on me. I know that's what they tell you to do first, but, I can only make one commitment at a time, and I need to make it to myself. I will keep the commitment between me and my willpower, and if I fall off the wagon a few times it's only me that can help myself climb back on again.

As difficult as it was for me to give up smoking, I did make it through (see **"MY CREDIBILITY ALMOST WENT UP IN SMOKE"** page 29). But looking back twenty years I know that I would do things differently today.

As for the dieting (again), everybody is aware when I start one. It's easy to notice I'm on my diet when I go out for lunch and only eat my friends' leftover carrots and tomatoes while acting like a frustrated crab. But, I no longer mention it to my family and friends.

The important thing is this—when I make a commitment, I make it only to myself. Then I take it one step, one day, at a time. This really works for me. Never say never, because this sounds too final, and that's what makes keeping my resolutions difficult. It means an end to something I've so thoroughly enjoyed, and the finality of that very word "never" is scary. I try telling myself that every day is a fresh start and a new beginning, and by believing in my own self, I can fulfill my dreams.

When I've reached my goals, I will show my loved ones and friends what I've accomplished. They will be very proud of me and admire my strength and willpower. But no one will be more satisfied than me.

The best part of all is that I did this with my own willpower, something that can't be bought or sold. I have succeeded in keeping my New Year's resolutions in the past, and this time I will stick to it again. When the next year starts to roll around, well. . . I'll think of a new goal to accomplish.

*Happy New Year!*